MEDJUGORJE

Editor Louise Hall

Medjugorje:
what it means to me

the columba press

First edition, 2012,
published by

the columba press

55A Spruce Avenue,
Stillorgan Industrial Park,
Blackrock, Co. Dublin

Cover by Bill Bolger
Cover image by Hrvoje Joe Topić
Origination by The Columba Press
Printed by MPG Print Group

ISBN 978 1 85607 805 4

Second Printing

The author would like to express her gratitude to photopraphers Hrvoje Joe Topić and Una Williams for kindly permitting the usage of their images. All other photographs taken from the Louise Hall collection.

List of Contributors

Foreword

This book containing the faith stories of pilgrims is a normal and natural development in the story of Medjugorje. One story creates another, and so on. The story that began on 24 June 1981 on the hillside of Bijakovići, in the parish of Medjugorje, in Bosnia and Herzegovina now continues in countries all over the world.

Today, in the year 2012, as I write these words, we celebrate the birthday of Our Lady. On that day when Our Lady was born the heavens spoke to the Earth and said: I love you. When Our Lady was born, the story of love between heaven and earth began in Christ. With Christ, our brother, and with Our Lady, our mother, we, the ordinary people – you and me – were called and became a heavenly family. The story of Our Lady and the story of Christ became the story of all in heaven and on earth. The heavens, as well as the earth, became our dwelling place.

As you read the words of this book, dear reader, I ask you to think of the gift God gave to the world in the person of Our Lady and in the person of Christ. But God does not stop there. The plan of love continues. When you were born there was the same plan of love in heaven. God thought of love and so he thought of you. God gave you to the world in love. When you were born God wanted the world to receive the greatest gift, the same gift given in the birth of Our Lady and in the birth of Christ. You are the gift of God to the world. God has the same plan and the same intention for you as for Christ and Our Lady. God wants every person to continue to be his gift to the world throughout their life until the end.

The story of the love of God began with the birth of Our Lady. It continues in every birth. It continues with every moment of life. The story of love continues in every sacrament, in every prayer and in every moment of faith. This story of the love of God continues with the story of Our Lady in Medjugorje.

In the biblical pages of the New Testament we read stories of people receiving Christ. In pilgrimage this biblical drama of faith continues as people encounter Christ in the sacraments. In a special way, this story of faith continues in the lives of people from Ireland, as this book witnesses. This book is a continuation of the biblical stories in our time. In *Medjugorje: what it means to me* we see the drama of Christ coming to his people as it happens in our time; before our very eyes. I strongly recommend this book. Everyone needs to be a story in it.

Fr Svetozar Kraljevic
Medjugorje,
September 2012

Introduction

On 24 June 1981, six young children claimed to have seen a vision of Our Lady on a small hill called Podbrdo in the poor Catholic farming village of Medjugorje. Although they ran away terrified at the sight of the apparition, they returned to the same spot at the same time the following day and came face to face with the mother of God, who has continued to appear to them every day since then. When the children asked Our Lady why she had appeared she answered, 'I have come to let you know that God does exist.'

Over thirty years later, in what is said by some to be a continuation of Lourdes and Fatima, more than 40 million curious pilgrims have descended on the quaint village of Medjugorje in Bosnia and Herzegovina, eager to hear what the 'Queen of Peace' has to say.

On the 25th of each month, the 'Gospa', as the visionaries fondly call her, gives a message to the world. The messages are of peace, love, reconciliation, fasting and prayer; and always begin with 'Dear Children' and end with, 'Thank you for having responded to my call.'

Many people, including journalists, have tried to discredit the allegations but most come home converted and eager to spread the messages they receive. The village of Medjugorje has now adapted to cope with the influx of tourists and continues to attract people of all religions from all over the world. When the church of St James (patron saint of pilgrims) was built in 1933 everyone thought it was far too big for the small village; little did they know that millions of pilgrims would pass through its doors many years later.

The large white cross on Mount Križevac is the first thing pilgrims see when they come to Medjugorje. It was also built in 1933 and contains a piece of the true cross of Christ.

The six visionaries, who are now grown adults with children of their own, still claim to see the Virgin Mary, albeit some less frequently than others. When people ask the six seers to describe the woman who appears they explain as best they can the incomparable beauty before their eyes.

According to the visionaries, the Madonna appears in a greyish-blue dress with a long white veil. Her hair is black and her eyes are blue and she floats on a white cloud; a crown of twelve gold stars sits comfortably on her head. On feast days and special occasions she dresses in gold, sometimes holding the baby Jesus in her arms. Other times, he is said to appear standing beside her with the crown of thorns torturing his bleeding head.

The visionaries say that when Our Lady appears a little piece of heaven comes with her and that if we knew how much Our Lady loved us, we would cry tears of joy.

Travelling out to Medjugorje for the 30th anniversary of the apparitions in 2011 brought me face to face with many Irish pilgrims. Each person was there for different reasons; some in thanksgiving for the good in their lives; others to pray for a sick relative or friend; more who were simply searching and hoping to awaken and reinstate the spirituality they were born with but may have lost along their journey through life.

Each and every person I met had an intriguing story to tell about how they were introduced to Medjugorje and why they felt drawn to travel there.

My mother brought the first group of Irish pilgrims out to the village back in the eighties and each one of her five children always accompanied her on the trips, including me.

As a curious and naïve child, I can remember Medjugorje as the poor farming village it was many years ago and have fond memories of feeling pure peace and love in the hospitality of the local people who eagerly opened their homes to the masses of visitors. The food and wine they placed on our table each night was fresh from the earth and, although they had little in terms of wealth or material goods, they willingly gave us everything they possible could.

The lack of wealth in the village was evident and, even though this was at a time during the eighties when Ireland was going through its own tough economic recession, I can still remember the generosity of the Irish pilgrims who dug deep into their pockets on the last day of their stay, eagerly making up a collection of coins and notes of both dollars and local currency to give to the host families as a token of appreciation for their hospitality.

I remember going back as a teenager to the Youth Festivals where a young and newly-ordained Fr Liam Lawton, along with Fr Slavko, who was spiritual advisor to the visionaries, were present, as were hundreds of young people from all over the world who were housed in twenty-man tents on the outskirts of the village where they engaged in a week of folk music, song and prayer. For me, it was like a spiritual and social uprising drenched in enthusiasm, faith and love. Here, I met many like-minded young people and I could leave behind all that was expected of me by my peers and detach myself from the, sometimes extreme, pressures and expectations which were associated with the turbulent teenage years. Medjugorje was a place where everyone was invited and accepted, regardless of one's failings and imperfections.

It is very true that once you visit Medjugorje you will undoubtedly return. People rarely travel there only once and the place possesses a strange, compelling magnetic effect. As I got older, I journeyed on through life, entered adulthood, fell in love and started a family and, though I always said I would return to Medjugorje, it never seemed to be the right time in my life to do so.

In 2008 my sister died very suddenly at the young age of twenty-six. She had accompanied my mother on her first trip to Medjugorje many years ago when she was only two years old. Nicky was born with Down's syndrome. She was the light of our life and our family was stricken with an indescribable and heart-wrenching grief when she passed away. Suddenly, I became very aware of my own mortality and made a conscious decision to stop putting off things in my life that I always wanted to do.

When I heard that Vicka was appearing on *The Late Late Show* in February 2011, I was fortunate enough to be a guest in the green room. My mother was also there and we all chatted amiably with Vicka, who I can only describe as the 'smiling visionary' who seems to have this constant light emanating from her.

Later on, Vicka and my mother shared a private moment together and my mother openly expressed her grief at the loss of my sister. Vicka listened on sympathetically, pure empathy evident in her eyes, and my mother listened attentively as the kind-hearted visionary told her how children with special needs are sent down as a gift from heaven. She said they are sent down to teach us and bring love. However, they are also called back, up to where they belong, to live in eternal happiness.

I made my decision that night to go back to Medjugorje for the 30th anniversary of the apparitions. I didn't know the real reason why I was going back. I just knew that I was giving in to that strong pull and desire to once again visit this holy place.

Before I travelled over, I was asked by the *Sunday Independent,* *Woman's Way* and the *Medjugorje Herald* to write for them while I was on the trip and so I knew my time was limited as I had deadlines to adhere to and many people to meet within five days.

Arriving at the village after more than twenty years, I was both surprised and encouraged to see that the authenticity of the village had remained intact despite the inevitable arrival of commercialism. I inhaled and soaked up the reverential and venerable ambiance and allowed myself to get lost amidst the undeniable sense of peace and love.

On my second day, I was lucky to get an interview with Ivan, one of the visionaries, as his schedule was consumed with radio and television interviews that week. Nevertheless, he agreed to meet me under the shade of a tree in the grounds of St James Church the morning after I arrived. He spoke through an interpreter called Daniela.

The married man reflected on the past thirty years by saying, 'These days, I really go back to the first date and I want to renew those first beginnings which are so profound in my memory. I want to filter all that was so amazing and so beautiful. For me and my wife, this truly has been a great gift.'

When I asked Ivan about the messages Our Lady had for the people, he was confident in his reply.

'When Our Lady speaks, she speaks to us all. She is our mother, she loves us all and we are all important to her; there are no rejected ones. She needs us to spread her message. That is why it is paramount that we realise the importance of her coming and of her messages during this moment and time we are living in.'

I asked him what the most important messages were.

'In a special way, I would like to emphasise the most important message which in my opinion is the message of peace and prayer. If we don't listen to those two, then we cannot accept all of the messages that Our Lady is sending. It is hard and difficult to forgive if you do not have peace in your heart. Without forgiveness there is no healing. If there is no spiritual healing, then there is no physical healing.'

Ivan finished off by saying that we must be free and open to the Holy Spirit and in that way we can accept what Our Lady desires for us.

The rest of my week was filled with stories and testimonies from different people from all walks of life and I absorbed the universal message of love and peace that emanated from every pilgrim in the village. It was almost indescribable and that familiar and welcoming feeling of enthusiasm, faith and love began to burn once again inside me. I also listened intently to various stories of events that have happened in the village in recent times. It was intriguing to hear of a group of young European students who, months earlier, were gathered around the white statue of Our Lady in the grounds of St James Church. A pilgrim had noticed that every person in the young group had tears flowing down their cheeks. When the pilgrim approached the group, she asked them why they were crying – assuming they must have lost a friend recently who was very close to them.

The students turned to the inquisitive pilgrim and said, 'Look. Can you not see? Our Lady; she is calling us closer.' They went on to explain that the hand of the statue had been moving, motioning them all to come nearer.

When I ventured up to the Blue Cross one sun-filled morning, passing through the picturesque vineyards with the ever present impressive mountains nestled comfortably in the backdrop, I sat on a rock at the foot of the cross and listened to a mesmerising story.

Our guide for the week explained how during the Bosnian War the soldiers wouldn't let the visionaries go to Apparition Hill. For the six children, it was torture not to see the Blessed Virgin and so Ivan decided to disobey the commands as he sneaked out of his home one evening. When he came to the foot of Podbrdo there was an old stone house over to the right and Ivan ventured over trying to be as quiet as he could. Suddenly, he heard Our Lady's voice and she told him that the soldiers were near by and that he must stay exactly where he was.

The guide continued to tell us that Ivan stood very still but within seconds, the sniffer dogs and soldiers were by his side. However, after a few moments they moved on past him. It is said that the Gospa made him invisible for those few moments.

While still sitting at the Blue Cross, the articulate guide told us that just the other day she was bringing another group of pilgrims up Podbrdo. She had been praying hard that week, despite her busy work schedule, and had achieved what she set out to do in terms of prayers and Mass. Pondering on her week, she wondered to herself who she should offer her prayers up for. Moments later she noticed a beautiful young family all dressed from head to foot in pristinely clean clothes, with pictures of Our Lady on their hats and T-shirts. The father had his back to the guide and held a young child in his arms. The mother, who the guide described as extremely pretty, had sunglasses on and was feeding an infant child in her arms.

When the mother took off her sunglasses, the guide said she felt baffled as to why this stunningly beautiful mother had such a sad look in her eyes. It was only seconds later, when the man turned around with the other child in his arms, that she realised the plight of the mother. The father held a young child, about two years of age, who was obviously very sick as he had many tubes coming out of his nose and mouth. Although her heart ached at the sight, the guide said she knew exactly where her prayers must be directed and offered everything from the past week up for this child and family.

It gave me some comfort that when we feel helpless in similar situations where neither words nor actions can change a person's fate, if nothing else, we can offer up a prayer for their plight.

On the day of the anniversary, I listened attentively to Fr Svet's homily where he spoke about the Cenacolo Community and the nun who founded the organisation which helps young men with addiction. I found his words to the listening congregation very apt: 'Let us all be apparitions to each other.'

Only earlier that day, I had visited the Merciful Fathers rehabilitation centre up at The Mother's Village and listened to the testimonies of two recovering addicts whose lives were torn apart by the effects of the Bosnian War. As chronic drug addicts, the Merciful Father's centre was their last hope and both were doing extremely well and receiving treatment through work and prayer. Later that day, I met with Bobbi, a former successful professional gymnast and thirty-time champion in Macedonia who also turned to heroin and began dealing drugs at fourteen years of age. When he broke his leg, leaving him unable to compete, and his parents divorced he became very depressed and turned to drink, marijuana and eventually heroin. At twenty-three years of age he went into the Merciful Fathers and began treatment. He was now clean for over four and a half years and working actively within the parish and church of St James.

When introduced to Arthur McCluskey, who hailed from the town of Emo, Co. Laois, I instantly became intrigued to hear about the story of his life. Arthur was a wealthy businessman but a self-confessed chronic gambler who would often lose thousands of pounds on the horses in a day. He gave his testimony on how Medjugorje changed his life to a houseful of pilgrims on the evening of the anniversary and his story left an impact on all who were listening.

* * *

It is true that we, as humans, are naturally curious about the afterlife and for me I feel that even the toughest of sceptics would find it difficult to ignore what has been going on in Medjugorje over the past thirty years.

From how they first came to find out about the small village and what was happening there to how they found themselves travelling to this place of pilgrimage, *Medjugorje: what it means to me* is a collection of testimonies from Irish people detailing the impact this intriguing little village had, and still has, on their lives.

What Medjugorje means to me can be summed up in the effortless love and goodness I have in my life today. I am eternally grateful to my mother for her natural curiosity which spurred her to travel to the village many years ago. Little did she know the grounding it would give me as a child for my journey through life and the impact it would have on me when I returned as a grown and mature adult over twenty years later.

Everyone takes their own meaning and understanding when visiting the village and, for me personally, I came to appreciate that man creates divides, not God. The visionaries once asked Our Lady who was the holiest person in the village? She named a local Muslim woman, explaining that she was the closest to God. Medjugorje is a place where everyone is embraced, regardless of creed. The messages are simply urging us to lead better lives so we can embrace and be fulfilled with the happiness God intended for us in this sometimes difficult journey through life.

A lady, whose testimony features in the book, put it very simply to me one day as we drove home from a mutual friend's funeral. I asked her why she thought Our Lady was appearing in Medjugorje. Her reply was poignant and heartwarming.

She told me that if she died and went to heaven and there was some way that she could come back and tell her children how best to live their lives, then she would do it. This is what she thinks Our Lady is doing and has been doing in Medjugorje for over thirty years: she is advising her children on how to live their lives.

Just as Ivan said, 'When Our Lady speaks, she speaks to us all. She is our mother.' We are all her children – and here are just some of our testimonies.

Louise Hall, Editor

1

Liam Lawton

Liam Lawton is a world-renowned composer and singer and is well known for his ministry of music, which has seen him perform on stage all over the world. It was in the village of Medjugorje that he found this ministry which now brings joy to thousands of music lovers worldwide.

This is Liam's testimony.

When I was a young priest in the seminary, I came across an English Catholic newspaper which was telling the story of what was happening in Medjugorje. I was instantly intrigued by the story, especially because of the fact that it was happening behind the Iron Curtain.

There was a whole political scenario surrounding it and it told in the newspaper of how difficult it was to get to the place both because of the geographical terrain and also because of the political ramifications. People simply weren't going in because it was annoying the authorities intensely.

It had only started in 1981 and after reading the newspaper, I heard nothing of it again until 1986. I met a couple from Dublin who mistook me for my twin brother. However, when they realised it was me they told me how they had been looking for me and that they would like me to come to Medjugorje.

They had already visited the place and wanted me to experience it for myself. I was fascinated and curious and made my decision there and then to go along with them.

We flew into Mostar which was a military airport and because I was a priest, the airport security guards took me aside and I was searched. I had also brought some food with me to give to the people I was staying with and all of it was immediately taken off me.

I can vividly remember a female army officer get extremely annoyed with me and she said, 'Do you not think we have food over here?'

They also took my prayer book and turned it upside down and shook it hard, as if they were trying to see what I had hidden in it.

When I arrived at the village I stayed with a lovely old couple and a grandmother. It was very basic and the people were so poor and it was a real typical reflection of how the Catholics in the area had nothing, simply because they had remained faithful to their faith and didn't become members of the Communist Party.

I was instantly moved by the natural devotion of the people and to me it was the biggest sign that something was most definitely happening here because despite all the terrible persecution, they were still going to the mountains to pray.

I met one guy called Ritzo who was only eighteen years old. He had been beaten so severely that he had gone into renal failure. The reason he was beaten was that he had continued to go to the mountain to pray after the soldiers had told him not to.

There was also an old grandmother called Baba Eva who was very elderly and couldn't walk. She would sit at the door praying all day long. Her smile was beautiful and her eyes were totally alive.

One day I spoke to her, through her granddaughter who could speak some English.

I asked her, 'Have you ever seen the Gospa?'

She was quite indignant with me and she answered by saying, 'Of course I have seen her!'

I asked her, 'When?'

She told me that she saw the Gospa on the Way of the Cross at night.

I had no reason to disbelieve this woman. Here she was sitting and praying all day and, for her, it was no problem at all to believe that this was happening, such was her astounding faith.

Back in the early days, the apparitions happened at the back of the church or in the priest's house.

I was fortunate to be present a few times during an apparition and there was a time when I felt so deeply moved and overcome with emotion. I felt there was a lot of healing taking place in my own personal life while I was there. I cried a lot during the apparition and couldn't seem to stop the tears from flowing.

Another thing that had a profound impact on me over there was the fact that being a priest, I was able to hear so many people's confessions. One man, who came into me, hadn't been to confession in forty-four years and felt drawn to go to Medjugorje. It seemed that while here, he felt the need and the want to go to a priest and talk about his life.

There was an awful lot of hurt in the country also, particularly about the Bosnian War. Medjugorje was a place that the people could go and visit. They were able to shed some of that hurt and talk about their lives again.

Over the years, I went back several times and I became very close to Fr Slavko. This particular priest was brought into the village to discredit and 'close down' the 'alleged' apparitions. Fr Slavko instantly believed what the six young children were saying and he was anxious to spread the word around to other priests so that they too would know and experience what was happening.

There were so many healings taking place back in the early days, both spiritual and physical. So many people who had previously doubted God's existence had realised over there that he did indeed exist. It was because of Medjugorje that I found the courage to begin to write sacred music as I had been ordained a number of years and had not been writing. Fr Slavko had invited me to sing there and through him I had some beautiful experiences which affected me profoundly.

My friendship with Slavko continued and we went on to set up the annual Youth Festivals where young people from all over the world gathered on the outskirts of the village in large tents for a week of music, song and prayer.

I was fortunate to meet a man called Ernest Williams who had a dream that young people would gather in prayer before the blessed sacrament. He spoke to Slavko about it and, after much planning, the first Youth Festival took place in the early nineties and still goes on today.

There was another significant time when I found myself in Medjugorje and that was when Fr Jozo returned to the village after being imprisoned in a communist jail for two and a half years.

The day he returned to the village I was present. He came out, he spoke to the people from the edge of the town, in the forest as he was not allowed enter into the church. The people were going crazy when he returned and there were many stories going around that he had converted the guards in the prison. I remember coming down from the mountain one night and we had Mass at midnight. It was celebrated on the foundations of the new outdoor altar that now exists covered by the Dome, behind the church. There were thousands present that night. It was very special to sing.

Another night, a massive storm saw heavy rain and dangerous slippery conditions, but we still decided to climb the mountain. Our Lady was appearing up there and when I got to the top, I held an umbrella over Ivan's head.

We were all soaked right through to our skin such was the force of the wind, thunder and rain.

During the apparition the sky seemed to split in two, the rain stopped almost instantly and millions of stars suddenly appeared in the clear night sky.

Ivan told the interpreter that when Our Lady departed, she held up her arms towards the sky. When we arrived at the bottom of the mountain, every one of us was completely dry.

When I think of Medjugorje, I feel that everybody is called there for one reason or another and you might not know why. Yet when you get there you can open your heart to God. No matter what your problem is, you have the experience that God is listening and that everything will be alright.

It can be very difficult when you come home but I will always remember the two local girls in Medjugorje, Jelena Vasilj and Marijana Vasilj, who were having inner locutions. This is where people experience hearing the voice of God from inside.

At a prayer meeting one night Jelena said that Our Lady had told them that many people will come to Medjugorje and they will receive beautiful gifts there but when they go home, they will forget about them. Jelena said that these are the people that will one day be most disappointed because they will have been offered something very special and they will have left it there.

When you visit Medjugorje, you really experience God's love for you. In a way, it reminds me of when the disciples went up to Mount Tabor. They desperately wanted to stay there and pitch up tents but Jesus knew he had to go back and face his crucifixion.

I always say to people that you can go to Medjugorje any day you want, in your heart. You can climb that mountain any time you want. It is nice to be there but not everyone gets the chance to go as often as they like.

The diversity of people who visit Medjugorje is amazing. People from all walks of life can be found there.

Medjugorje is a place devoid of cynicism. I feel we have become very cynical in Ireland, for a variety of reasons. But when you go there, there is you and God and there is the mountain. You have the church, the hills and the vineyards and to me it is the most peaceful and prayerful place in the world today. There are huge graces over there and most people experience the sacrament of Reconciliation.

So many Irish people have been to Medjugorje and I feel they need to stand up and be witness to their faith because sometimes we are not too good at that here.

Medjugorje gave me a better relationship with Mary on a much more human level. My journey was an interior one where I learned a greater appreciation of the rosary, as a mantra and in the form of prayer. It gave me a greater appreciation of the Eucharist and helped me go deeper into prayer.

There are so many temptations out there, especially within the entertainment industry and it is not always easy to resist them. However, I always found that Medjugorje grounds you, supports you and consoles you. It is a place that has brought many great blessings into my life.

I have seen so many people's lives touched and changed by Medjugorje. Our Lady said that she will come to every home, to let people know that God exists and she is doing that all the time.

What does it mean to me?

To me, Medjugorje is a sign to the world that God exists in a world that doesn't always want to hear that. I think it is a place of deep, deep healing both on a spiritual and physical level. There are over 600 documented physical healings and Cenacolo rehabilitation centre for addicts has a ninety-seven per cent success rate.

Many priests have rediscovered their vocation there. More people have experienced the sacrament of Reconciliation there, and the graces that come from this are huge.

It has brought many wonderful people into my life which is extremely important to me as it puts me in contact with like-minded people who can support me, particularly in difficult times.

You judge a place by its fruits and Medjugorje has fruits in abundance. It also wants and needs the people to have the courage to stand up and say: 'Yes, God exists.'

2

Mary Kennedy

Mary Kennedy is a well-known TV presenter with RTÉ. Mary visited Medjugorje for the first time in 2008 and then filmed in the village with Nationwide for the 30th anniversary of the apparitions.

This is Mary's testimony.

I visited Medjugorje for the first time in 2008. I went with an open mind and really knew very little about the place before travelling. Fatima and Lourdes were the Marian shrines that I was familiar with growing up. And of course Knock, but that was close to home and didn't have the same exotic feel to it as did the mainland European destinations.

When I arrived in the village of Medjugorje for the first time, I immediately warmed to the place, despite the fact that it was pouring rain, and I was looking forward to a week of June sunshine as part of the deal. What appealed to me was the simplicity of the place. The fact that I had to walk through the fields and rural settings to get to the small mountain, or Apparition Hill as it is better known, was a wonderful experience in itself.

Along the way, I passed small, simple rural houses which were very quaint, among them the homes of the visionaries and their families. The scenery was both breathtaking and unspoiled, with wide open spaces to trek through and the vista of mountains and hills in the distance. The full expanse of the landscape came into its own on the third day when the clouds lifted and the rain cleared. That was a magical moment and there's no doubt that you appreciate something more when you have to wait for it, including heat and sunshine!

I stayed in one of the local homes which was situated down a quiet side street not too far from St James Church. It was a bit like being in the Gaeltacht in a way because during the day, when I was out and about, people would stop and ask, 'Whose house are you staying in?'

The food was wonderful, simple, fresh and wholesome and the family was friendly and hospitable. All the guests ate together at long tables. Marina, the *bean a' tí*, and her husband would stand up in front of the pilgrims and lead us all in Grace before meals. In a way, it was like stepping back in time.

It reminded me of growing up in Clondalkin when the whole family would sit down to dinner or tea and say Grace before starting to eat. It doesn't happen a lot these days and it was a lovely precursor to meals in Medjugorje; a nice, gentle way of giving thanks for good and abundant food and an opportunity to focus on the fact that someone had taken the trouble and the care to prepare this food.

During that first visit to Medjugorje in 2008, I met Maria, one of the visionaries. I was part of a group that was invited to her house for coffee. I found her warm and quite ordinary and normal. She had a little purpose-built chapel in her garden and it was packed with many people, mostly Italians, who wanted to see where she prays while she's at home in Medjugorje because she now lives most of the time in Italy with her Italian husband and four sons.

I admired the fact that Maria was a woman who was married and had a family and that she has a central role in all that's happening in Medjugorje. This reality underlines for me the truth that you don't have to live a life of celibacy and be childless in order to be in the top rank of closeness to God.

A priest friend of mine once said that he could never believe that all those years ago Jesus decided that he was going to form an all-male club. I couldn't agree more and the presence of strong women with deep faith in this part of the world where millions of people come to pray and find comfort is a positive and welcome sign in these times of turmoil in the Catholic Church.

The question that is constantly asked, of course, is whether or not the apparitions actually happen. I don't know the answer to that.

When I returned to Medjugorje in 2011 to film a special edition of *Nationwide* to mark the 30th anniversary of the start of the phenomena, I met Ivan and was present during his apparition. I found it a very tranquil and holy experience; one that was prayerful, peaceful and respectful.

I also met and interviewed Mirjana, who I found to be really beautiful and gentle. I put it to her that there were many people who would consider her to be 'bonkers', that asking people to believe that Mary appears to her and her fellow visionaries was the same as asking people to believe in magic.

She replied by asking me if I thought that, growing up over the past thirty years, as a teenager, then as a young woman getting married, it was a blessing to have all that publicity, investigation and lack of privacy?

She explained that it wasn't something she would have chosen in life but it happened and she could not deny the responsibility that had been given to her and her friends. That to me was very encouraging. I believe that this is all very real for the visionaries and I feel that they have given so much consolation and hope to many people around the world.

One of the many special places in Medjugorje is St James Church in the centre of the main street. It is the focal point for all pilgrims and there are Masses and other services there at different times of the day. The evening celebration of the Eucharist has to be seen to be believed.

It is celebrated behind the church in a purpose-built dome and there are literally thousands of people in the congregation every evening. They sit in the outdoor pews, on the grass, on the paths, anywhere there is a little bit of space. The atmosphere is peaceful, prayerful and tranquil. People are there because they want to be there. You would hear a pin drop, such is the reverence and stillness.

There are no stewards present. There is no security. It is not needed. I can't think of any other situation in the world where you could have a crowd that size without a significant level of policing and security.

Apparition Hill was certainly my favourite place in the village, perhaps because of the simple way of getting to it that I described earlier, the walk out of the village through the fields and passing by the rural dwellings. There's another reason though that I enjoyed going to the hill. This is where the pilgrims go to say the rosary. It's a gentle climb and the decades of the rosary are depicted on beautifully crafted bronze plaques.

Being on Apparition Hill brought back nice memories to me of my childhood. I grew up in a family where we said the rosary every single evening after tea. We'd just be finishing off the meal and looking forward to getting out to play with the pals and then we'd hear my mother saying, 'Hand me down the beads,' and we all knew what was coming next. I would be lying if I said we didn't all dread those words and I can remember keeping an eye out for possible visitors to our house which meant we might get out of the daily ritual.

Since I have come home from Medjugorje, I have embraced the rosary again. I like to say it when I'm out walking. I offer it up for any intention in my heart and I know my mother, after all my protestations as a child, would be very pleased

For me, Medjugorje is a prayerful, peaceful and wholesome place. You don't have to lock yourself away in prayer for the whole time. There's a very pleasant social aspect to a visit to Medjugorje also. There are lovely coffee shops and restaurants, great hairdressers at a fraction of the price we pay here, excellent holistic massage opportunities and nice shops, most with religious artifacts but also some good shoe shops and craft shops for instance.

Medjugorje is a very popular place with Irish pilgrims. I met people from all walks of life and from all parts of the country when I was there. In 2011, I met a group of six men who are golfing buddies. One of them had lost his wife and the others decided that they would all go to Medjugorje with their friend. They were great company, enjoyed the spiritual comfort they found there and the time out from their daily routine.

It's a very sociable place, a great place to unwind and focus on the important things in life. People are nice to each other and helpful. There's a lovely spirit of community. When you go to morning Mass, you are surrounded by people from all around the world, people who have come to Medjugorje to be their best and to do their best.

There is a piece in the Old Testament from the Book of Micah (6:8) which sums up, for me, the way I would like to live my life and I have to say that following a visit to Medjugorje, it seems that bit easier to do so:

Act justly,
Love tenderly,
And walk humbly with your God.

3

Shaun Doherty

Shaun Doherty is the presenter of The Shaun Doherty Show *on Highland Radio in Donegal. The popular radio host travelled out to Medjugorje for the first time in September 2011 and the village has had a lasting impact on his life ever since.*

This is Shaun's testimony.

My first introduction to Medjugorje came very early on in the whole story. I began my broadcasting career twenty-two years ago and within the first year I can vividly remember being approached by people who had come back from there, full of enthusiasm for the place.

I would have known more about Lourdes and Fatima, as I had been to Lourdes as a child. The people who were speaking of Medjugorje were very enthused and this interested me.

Not too long after, one of the visionaries came to Letterkenny with Fr Slavko, their spiritual director. It was Maria and I interviewed her through a translator. It was a nice experience and I found her very ordinary. Maria gave me a medal before she left.

That was how my first interest in Medjugorje began and through the years, from time to time, people would call into the show and talk about an experience they had there. They talked about the phenomena of the sun spinning out there and other miracles that had happened.

There was no doubt that Medjugorje would feature on the show from time to time. However, when the Bosnian war broke out I didn't really hear anything because nobody was going. It seemed to have fallen flat in terms of media interest and it was only when the war ended and people started to go again that I began to hear more about it.

Personally, I wasn't too interested. It was just there and there were times when I wondered if there really was anything real about it at all.

Through the years stories began to emerge that the visionaries were becoming very wealthy. There was one story in particular circulating about one of the visionaries wearing a Rolex watch. That was in the back of my mind and I started to get a bit cynical. Those kinds of stories had a tendency to feed your disbelief and your cynicism of these places.

There was no real discussion about Medjugorje in my life after that up until about three years ago.

I wanted a bit of help, through prayer, to help me get through this difficult time in my life. I made a promise to myself, that if I got through it and received that help that I would go to Medjugorje. I don't know why I picked Medjugorje and not Lourdes or Fatima but, like a lot of promises in your head and good intentions you make, I didn't keep it.

Two years passed by and in September 2011, I was sitting in work doing my daily show and I felt a real need of a break. One of the staff, Greg, who would usually fill in for me, came in and I asked him if he could cover as I needed to take a week off. He said to me, 'You are already off from tomorrow, you put in for it a while back.' I had completely forgotten about it and it was like being given Christmas as I was really ready for a break.

I went home that day and my sister Margaret and her husband Joe were staying with me but were due to go home to England over the next couple of days. Immediately I went online and looked for flights to Medjugorje. I found a flight that was leaving from Leeds but had no accommodation booked. I got on the ferry with my sister and her husband, got the train from Manchester down to Leeds, stayed overnight in Leeds and was on a plane the next day on my way to Medjugorje.

In the meantime I was asking one of the staff at the radio station to check with a man whose daughter was living out there if he could sort out some accommodation for me. I was told to stop off at Paddy Travel and all would be sorted.

When the plane landed, I was collected by a man called Ivan and taken to the village.

The accommodation was lovely, very simple and only a 5-minute-walk from the church. My first impression of the village was that it was very small and was not what I was expecting. Compared to Lourdes, I found it a very different experience. When I went into St James Church, I remember thinking how small it was, even though it was considered quite large for such a small village.

After visiting the church, I decided to go straight up to Apparition Hill. It was getting close to dark and I really had no idea where to go. I didn't know what was there, what I was supposed to do or not do or what was even expected of me. Nevertheless, I climbed up the hill.

When I reached the top, there were about four people there and it was getting further into the evening. The statue of Our Lady was all lit up in white. I sat down on a rock and I remember getting this lovely sense of peace. I began thinking about things and I was happy in my thoughts.

A group of young guys came up, who were probably from the Cenacolo community. They all knelt down at the one spot and started praying. They then stood up and walked on. The men looked like they were all between twenty and thirty years of age and what really struck me and impressed me was the prayerfulness and respect they displayed.

My journey began then and from that moment I felt my problems and worries were easing away.

There were ups and downs over the next few days. One minute I was feeling that everything was great and then other times I began to question it all as I wasn't really seeing anything happening. It was a true reflection of my life at that time and I knew this was something I needed to ride through.

While out in the evenings, what really struck me about the village was the reverence of the local people, who would stand around with their rosary beads. Some would have little radios held up to their ears, as the Mass was transmitted through this medium, and they could all be seen to be in deep prayer.

I remember feeling that I couldn't think of another place in the world where prayer and God was so much a part of the people's lives – both visibly and privately. I felt that this must have been Ireland many years ago, back in my grandparents' time. These people had this for thirty years and they were still praying. The old people that I was looking at were probably in their forties when the apparitions had all started and it was obviously still hugely important to them.

People had spoken to me about the commercialism of Medjugorje and all the shops that have sprung up there, but this aspect never bothered me because I loved going around the shops as it was a little distraction. I didn't want to be praying 24/7 and I loved buying little relics to bring home as gifts.

It made sense to me that wherever there was an influx of tourists there are always going to be people who wanted to buy. When I got home, and gave my gifts to various people, I couldn't believe how much they meant to them. There are many people who have become very cynical about religion and you would think that they wouldn't think much of a religious object but I didn't hand anything to anybody who wasn't extremely appreciative of it.

Since then, some young people who had never said the rosary before have come up to me and said, 'Shaun, I have started to say the rosary with those beads you gave me.' I remember giving a man in his seventies a little card from Medjugorje to put in his wallet and he cried because it meant so much to him. This proved to me that people still have a great yearning for their faith and love for God.

It is wonderful to see how people honour Mary and feel she is a great advocate to go to and request special favours from God, through prayers. I found that for the priests in Medjugorje the central focus was God through Mass, with Our Blessed Mother encouraging us to a stronger belief.

I would challenge anybody to go to the Holy Hour at the back of the Dome at night where the blessed sacrament is exposed and not be moved by the entire experience. I felt a really strong presence of heaven meeting earth at this place.

No matter where you are in your faith, it is a beautiful hour where you can totally get into the zone and leave the world. There is a famous violinist who came to discover Medjugorje and she ended up staying there playing her wonderful music at night.

People talk about going off and playing golf and leaving the worries of the world behind them. Medjugorje to me is like a religious golf course. When you are there, you don't think about what is happening in the world. You focus on enjoying the time that you are there.

You need that space and that time to nourish you and help you go back and face the world with all its highs and lows. I remember coming back from Medjugorje the first time feeling very happy. Problems I had gone with, I came back without.

As a young person I would have had a very strong faith. My mother was very devout and very decent, good and kind-hearted. She had a very hard life but loved her faith yet was non-judgemental at the same time. I remember she would take me to the novenas every Wednesday night. The feeling I had over in Medjugorje would have been very similar to the feeling I would have had as a child practising my faith.

Since I have come home, I have much more of an appreciation of the Mass and its importance. I'm quieter in my faith in that I would stay silent and ask God to help me focus during Mass and in prayer for that time. Medjugorje gives you that focus.

Six weeks after my first visit to Medjugorje, I went back again and I have been there a third time since. I had time off work and I really wanted to go back. There was nowhere else I would rather go for a rest and a retreat.

I have heard so much from people about their experiences of Medjugorje and it is amazing how people identify with the exact same experiences. Everybody can't be wrong.

After I came home from my first visit, I remember being in my bed and awakening at about 2 a.m. For some reason, I had this song in my head and I thought to myself that I must write down what I was thinking. I wrote down the words to this song which I had never done before in my life and moments later I had the tune. I hummed the tune and recorded it on my mobile phone and within a few minutes, I had a song finished.

I went into two guys in Letterkenny called Timmy and Tommy, who own Full Tilt Studios. They would have been more used to young pop music and they are DJs on the dance music scene. Tommy Conway helped me and although he had never been to Medjugorje he was completely enthusiastic about the song.

His mother was working in the local Veritas store and she loved the song so much that she sold the CD through the shop. Within a few weeks we had sold 500 copies and were sold out.

The lyrics of the song 'The Call of Our Lady of Peace' were, of course, inspired by Medjugorje and it really tells my own personal story. So many people have told me how they can relate to it. It is also available on iTunes and all proceeds go to White Oaks, a centre founded by Fr Neil Carlin and the Columba Community for Addiction Problems.

Father Neil has been really helpful to me since I came back. Our journey goes back a long time to when I first came to Derry at 19 years of age. Columba house was just opened on Queen Street in Derry back then and the blessed sacrament is exposed there every day.

I saw the building and was curious, so I decided to go in. Father Neil was in there and we spoke. Twenty-six years later he remembered me coming into the house that day. He remembered putting his arm on my shoulder and praying with me. He told me that when he saw me in the house all those years ago that he saw good things ahead for me. He has been a tremendous support to me since I came home from Medjugorje and has become my spiritual guide. He has many gifts, including healing.

Everyone has times in their lives when they need a bit of help. We all have stresses in our life and I want the song to give people a bit of hope and help them realise that, no matter how bad things get in your life, God is there and he will lift you up.

There is a line in the song that says, 'lifted me up from my knees', and that is exactly how I felt when I went over to Medjugorje. I was so stressed and feeling low and down but I came back feeling lightened and lifted.

Medjugorje has become my favourite place. People need time and space, out of what they are doing and for some, a sun holiday simply doesn't do it. If you go to Medjugorje, you get it all and feel spoiled rotten.

The last time I was over in March 2012, I was sitting in the church and a woman and her son sat beside me. I remember thinking that they were Irish but I don't know why. We carried on in the Mass and we didn't speak until the sign of peace and after the Mass I went over to Columba's café across the street. Soon afterward, the woman's son came in and then she came in behind him. I looked at her and she smiled at me.

I said to her, 'Excuse me, are you from Donegal?'

She laughed and replied, 'Oh my God, it's you, Shaun Doherty!'

She started to sing my song to me and told me how her friends all thought she was mad because every time she answered the phone she was singing that song.

'The song means so much to me and I cannot believe you are here,' she said and then told me that she used to pray that one day I would come to Medjugorje.

Her name was Josephine and both her and her son had been going to Medjugorje for years. We became very friendly and began to see a lot of each other throughout the trip. We had great experiences on that particular third trip and I definitely made two friends for life.

What would have put me off before was when people came back from places such as Medjugorje and were too enthused about the whole experience. I found it fanatical and you would begin to think that these people were mad. Now I understand why they were so enthused and why people want to share in their experiences. They feel it is wrong to keep it to themselves. If you knew Tesco was giving away free food then naturally you would want to tell everyone.

I would defy anyone to sit in a room with ten people who have spent time in Medjugorje and hear their stories, their conversions and how their lives have turned around and then tell me that there is not something happening over there.

If you are going out to see the sun spinning or visions, then you may or may not be disappointed. It was never about that for me. I went because I knew instinctively that it would be a peaceful place to go and have a break. The rewards came and I don't believe that anyone will go to Medjugorje and not receive something.

What does Medjugorje mean to me?

Hardly a day goes by when I don't think about Medjugorje. Not just the place but what it means. It confirmed to me that God exists and that he is good, loving, merciful and compassionate. He will take you where you are at – no matter where – and help you.

It doesn't matter who you are or what you have done, there is nobody that can't be helped.

4

Arthur McCluskey

When I was introduced to Arthur McCluskey, by a priest in our group during the pilgrimage in 2011, I instantly became intrigued by the story of his life.

At six o'clock on 25 June 2011, a group of eager pilgrims gathered to hear this strong and kind-faced man give his testimony.

On 12 August 2011, I received a phone call from Arthur who thanked me for inviting him to the house to speak with the pilgrims and he said he hoped to meet me again in Medjugorje in years to come.

He died the following day.

With the permission of his family, this is Arthur's testimony.

I come from a place called Emo in Co. Laois. My father was a school teacher and I was the seventh of eight children. In 1964, I emigrated to Scotland and I lived in Glasgow for thirty-six years. For twelve of those years living in Glasgow, I came back regularly to Ireland and played GAA for Emo and sometimes for Co. Laois. I then returned to live in Ireland in 1999.

In 1971, I set up my own furniture and mail order business and within a short space of time it became very successful. I had a string of racehorses and a very different lifestyle. I regularly flew Concorde and first class travel around the world. Money was absolutely no object. But in the midst of all this grandiose lifestyle, I was also a compulsive gambler on racehorses, often losing in excess of 30,000 pounds sterling a day. It was a lot of money and you can imagine the value of it then; it was huge.

Over the years, my attitude towards the church had cooled somewhat. I felt the priests were saying one thing from the pulpit and practising another. I was only an occasional churchgoer; usually going only when my mother came to visit me. I put on a great act, especially when I went home to Ireland. I had been to confession only once in thirty years.

In 1981 my brother Eamonn came and joined my furniture business in Glasgow, after a successful career in Hotel Management and after a failed marriage. Three years later, he died. I went into the hospital the day after he had been rushed in and spoke with the consultant.

He told me that one lung and two vertebrae had been eaten away by cancer and they couldn't operate on him for fear of paralysing him. When I asked him the question of how long he had left to go, the answer was six months.

I was absolutely shattered by the news. I went home to try and gather my thoughts together before I went to see him to give him the information. I got a phone call five hours later to say that he died. I was devastated, especially because we had a falling out a short time before this happened. But I thanked God for taking him like he did because it would have been very hard for Eamonn, my mother and the family to see him endure a slow death.

About twenty minutes after the phone call from the hospital, I was at his bedside. I removed the white sheet from over his head and prayed the Act of Contrition into his ear. I then knelt down to pray some Hail Marys. It was like listening to the words through an earpiece; the words were spoken very, very slowly. After three Hail Marys I felt I knew the meaning of the prayer.

Some time after Eamonn was buried, I met a family friend in Tullamore called Eleanor McFadden and she showed me a video of Medjugorje and some girl having a vision. After I watched the video, I felt I might go there some day.

So of course, I went back to Scotland and wasn't going to church or anything. About five years later, I met Eleanor again and this time she gave me a set of white rosary beads. Of course, when I got back to Glasgow, I took the beads and dumped them in a dressing table drawer. I had no need for rosary beads in my lifestyle.

I was telling an ex-girlfriend about the beads and she told me that she had a friend in Dublin whose rosary beads had changed colour. She had a very mischievous grin on her face and said to me, 'You better keep an eye on them just in case.'

And I must admit that a couple of times during the year I would look in the dressing table drawer, just to see if the white rosary beads had turned blue because that was the other colour I associated Our Lady with from seeing pictures and statues.

At a family wedding in 1999, Eleanor's husband, Joe McFadden, came to me and asked me would I like to go to Medjugorje in June.

I said, 'What a great idea Joe, I would love to go.' But this was 1.30 a.m. and I was six sheets to the wind and when I came round the following afternoon, I hadn't the slightest intention of going to Medjugorje.

When I got back to Glasgow, I checked my diary and I had the perfect excuse for not going to Medjugorje because I had already invited three of my Scottish friends to play golf in Co. Kerry.

When I rang Joe to tell him, he said, 'Arthur, the very man, I was just about to call you. I got the dates wrong for Medjugorje. We are now going on the 23rd of June. Can you go then?'

I once again checked my diary and found myself saying, 'Yes, Joe, I can go then.' I put the phone down and I can tell you that the language I used was dreadful and asked myself, 'Why didn't I tell him a lie and get it over and done with?' I didn't want to tell a lie but I had a big business and I figured something would crop up.

To cut a long story short, because I have to move on … about a week before my departure, I was out having lunch with an architect friend of mine called Charlie Smith. He was a Presbyterian. I was telling Charlie about my regret and Charlie said, 'You know, if I was you, I would go. It might do you some good.'

Now that's not what I was expecting Charlie to say to me. He was a very good friend and I knew he spoke from the heart.

So then I decided that a week would fly by and I would go. I was packing my bags the night before my departure in Glasgow and I was being prompted to bring the white rosary beads with me.

When I was in the taxi, I phoned my friends from Dublin and told them where I was going. They said, 'What! You, of all people, going on a pilgrimage!' They couldn't believe it.

When I got to the airport, Eleanor introduced me to some of the group and I soon found myself being asked by people whether or not I had been to Lourdes or Fatima. I found myself asking, 'What am I going to do for a week with this group of potential pilgrim holidaymakers?'

I met a woman on the plane who said it was her fifth time going to Medjugorje and she loved going and that Our Lady touched her in a special way. I told her that I didn't know why I was going, that I don't even know how to pray.

The lady told me that she would be very surprised if I was saying that by the end of the week. Then I said that I would be very surprised if I was still there by the end of the week!

When we arrived at Medjugorje, we met up with another small group from Dundalk led by a man named Nicky.

The following morning, Eleanor decided to bring the group across the fields to Podbrdo. The group was praying on the way over and I had the rosary beads in my pocket. I wouldn't take them out in case someone saw me because I thought my reputation would be ruined!

On the way over, she pointed to the bigger hill in the distance and said it was Mount Križevac or Cross Mountain. Eleanor also mentioned something about the Blue Cross and one of the visionaries and all I could think about was, 'What have I got myself in for; how did I end up here and how do I get out of it?'

We went to Blue Cross and everyone started to pray but after a while I just left the group – I had had enough. There were thousands of people around and it was 24 June, so it was the Feast Day of St John the Baptist. I just thought everyone was a religious nut!

I ran off the hill and headed straight for a bar and had a few beers. I was trying to work out a way to tell Eleanor that I would catch up with the group at the end of the week at Split airport.

I noticed Nicky, the group leader from Dundalk and suddenly, without being invited, he plonked himself down beside me and he said, 'This is my fourth time in Medjugorje.'

He told me that I was here to meet a woman and I laughed to myself. I certainly chased women in my time but this was a different story. I told Nicky that I had been away from the Church for some time and he told me that his own mother had always been praying for him and his older brother. When I plucked up the courage to ask him what happened to the left side of his body, he told me he had a stroke at the age of nine. At that time his parents had taken him to Lourdes in the hope of a cure but he said that on his third trip to Medjugorje, Our Lady had touched him in a special way.

When he got home to Dundalk, he was on a high and was telling everyone about it but people were saying, 'All we hear from you is Medjugorje, Medjugorje, Medjugorje, but it hasn't cured you.' But he said it had, it had touched him here, as he touched his heart.

I had pitied Nicky when I met him first, seeing him limping around and thinking to myself, that poor eejit, going to Medjugorje looking for a cure and I would spend more on champagne than he gets in disability benefit. Yet here he was, twenty-four hours later, telling me about an inner healing and I wanted to talk more with him, so I did.

Over the next few days I wanted to hear what the visionaries had to say. By the second day, I realised that I wanted to do things.

At six o'clock the following morning, I set off from the house and headed across the vineyards towards Apparition Hill. I had the beads in my hand and I was praying the rosary for the first time in about forty years. Tears started to flow and I began crying like a child. I was looking up at the sky thinking: 'I'm an ex-GAA player and ex-rugby player. I'm much more macho than this.'

I continued walking and praying and crying and then some strange, mysterious things happened. I wasn't sure if I was taking the right path to the hill because it disappeared from view. I could see Cross Mountain very clearly and I could see the church but it was very far away. Three days after that, I discovered that I was having a vision of the church and that was when I was standing by the cross at Cross Mountain, which is 1,600 feet in the air.

I went on my way back to the main road and eventually came to the base of Cross Mountain. I knew nothing about Cross Mountain or about it having anything to do with the Stations of the Cross. All I could see was a path and I followed it.

I continued and when I came to Station number three, I heard what sounded like a branch breaking. I turned to see what it was and the trees behind the cross were shimmering and I thought I could see a face coming out. When I turned back again I saw an old lady standing about six feet to the left of the cross, waving at me and smiling. There wasn't a breath of air out that morning and when I turned again the leaves were still shimmering and she had a broad smile on her face. She was still waving and so I nodded my head to her.

I then continued up to the top and when I got there, there was a huge gathering at the cross so I went down to a quiet spot to try and pray the rosary. I was still crying all the time as I tried to pray. So I decided to go back down to the area where I saw the old lady at the Station. I was just about to leave there when I heard a female voice from behind the bushes and then I heard myself say, 'Who are you? Are you the mother of God?'

With that she seemed to fly over the bushes and she was in my arms in an instant and she invited me to sit on a rock beside her and she gave several strings of rosary beads to me which were replicas of the ones Eleanor had given to me ten years earlier.

They were all white except one set which were blue. I took the blue set and felt they were a special gift from our Blessed Mother. Then the old lady tapped me on my shoulder and said, in her own language, we will pray for each other, you for me and me for you. I was looking at my feet because I was trying to concentrate really hard on praying and the numbers 666 shot up to me from the lapels of my shoes.

A shiver went through my spine and I instantly felt that this was connected with Satan but I only realised the significance of those numbers later on.

After we finished praying, I gave her a hug and she told me of her many problems, including that she had a sore leg. I told her mine were spiritual. I wished her well and left with the feeling in my heart that something wonderful had happened to me.

It was only 9.30 in the morning and I knew confessions didn't start until the evening and I felt it was an awfully long time to wait. I told Nicky of my experiences and he stayed with me all day to make sure I got confession later on.

I went home to my house and, at a quarter to five, I went back over to the church and prayed at the statue of Our Lady outside St James' and asked for her help with my confession. I knew I wanted to go to confession to keep Satan out of my life.

Then I got into the queue and couldn't believe the amount of people who seemed to be taking ages in the confession.

I was thinking, 'What in the name of God are they telling? Will I ever get in?' I was being prompted all the time to go tomorrow, go tomorrow, even when it was my time to go into confession. I took off my dark glasses and told the priest, who I later realised was Fr Svet, it had been twenty years since my last confession and he asked me,

'Well, how are you?'

All the apprehension I had about going suddenly disappeared thanks to that beautiful man. I told him all about what happened on that morning, about the old lady and then I confessed my sins. I went and did my penance and then I met Nicky and we danced around the streets of Medjugorje.

Nicky told me that the following day he was going to climb Mount Križevac as a thank you to Jesus for my conversion. I went along with the group.

A priest told me that it was not expected that most of the group would get to the top but I was so very grateful to hear that they all made it and it reminded me of the monumental effort Jesus made for all of us when he was crucified.

Then my heart went out to the Blessed Mother for all the pain she went through, having to watch these painful scenes of her son. I began to admire priests and how their prayers were making each station come alive to me as we got to the top.

The next morning three of us set out to climb Apparition Hill.

I felt for Nicky but he told me that the previous year he had a problem climbing down the hill and fell on his side. He said to Jesus, 'There is no way I'll be seeing you tomorrow.' With that, he felt an invisible force lift his left paralysed arm and guide him down the hill.

The next day I climbed Križevac again and as I was at the third Station a male voice whispered in my ear, 'You will be at Cross Mountain on your own.'

There were lots of people praying at each Station but when I got to the top, everyone moved back from the cross and went away.

I found myself alone and I went forward and put my hands at the base of the cross. I heard myself say, 'Jesus, I'm yours forever,' and then the cross came alive in my hand.

It was as if it was flesh and I could feel Jesus going through his pain. Then I heard a deep voice and an Act of Contrition was said over me at the Cross. A sensation went through my body and I stood up and felt a great peace in my heart. I felt like I had been given a new heart. I looked down and saw the church and realised it was the vision I had seen three days earlier. Our Lady had led me to her son on Cross Mountain and he in turn had pointed me to his father in the church.

I prayed at the cross for some time and then went down to Station number three and stayed there for way over an hour. Everything since I had arrived in Medjugorje had turned full circle and I felt like I was in heaven on earth.

I went back to Glasgow and told all my friends about Medjugorje and then I got very strong feelings that I should go back to Ireland and look after my mother. I also wanted to help others, especially young people.

My mother, despite being 87, was still very independent and was able to drive. When I rang my mother, she told me that the previous day she set out and had only driven fifty yards when she had to stop, she had lost all confidence to drive and she then told me it would be wonderful if I came home.

I brought my mother out to Medjugorje that September and when she came out of the confessional box she had Fr Svet on her arms.

When I went into confession, Fr Svet told me that the prayers I experienced coming through the cross on my previous visit were due to my mother's prayers over the years.

I now live my life through prayer, peace, confession and fasting. I pray on average three hours a day. And every day I pray to the immaculate heart of the Blessed Mother, to thank her for pointing me in the direction of her son Jesus. And each day, I also pray to the Sacred Heart of Jesus to thank him for guiding me in the direction of his Father in the church, and for the peace and contentment and happiness that I have in my heart.

In October 1999, I sold off what needed to be sold off with my businesses. I still have a hotel in Aberdeen, Scotland.

On the boat back to Ireland, I heard a voice in my head saying: 'Start a charity.' My response was that I didn't know where to start especially after being out of the country for so many years. Subsequently, I got invited to go around Ireland with a man called Wayne Weible and I became a director for a charity called Rebuild for Bosnia, which helps families who lost everything during the war.

I loved the work and I thought this is what God wanted me to do. But after about three years or so I was being led in a different direction and so I decided to form my own charity called St Joseph and the Helpers.

So far we have been involved in building two schools, a nursing home and an orphanage and also St Joseph's Hall up in the Mother Village. We help and support 350 orphans on a regular basis and we are also involved in prosthetics.

You may think there is a lot of wealth in Medjugorje but a mile or so outside of the village there are many orphans and much poverty and we try to help all those affected. So that is the type of work I was led into.

As I said earlier, I was a chronic gambler and through the years I never admitted it to anybody. I also wrecked a business that had over one hundred employees and I never accepted any responsibility at all for that.

After feeling the Cross in my hands and praying there, I told Jesus I was addicted to gambling on the horses and I asked him to cure me, and from that day I never once gambled again and never had a taste for alcohol again. I knew with the help of Jesus I could get over it. I laugh about the fact that at the Feast of Cana he turned water into wine, but with me, he turned the wine into water.

I also wrote a book about my experiences called *My Healing from Gambling and Alcohol in Medjugorje* and all proceeds go to the orphanage. So far, it has raised over sixty thousand euro. The book can be purchased at the Mother Village or at the Medjugorje Centre.

Arthur's family wish to say the following:

It was undoubtedly Arthur's intention that those involved in the charity would continue to raise funds to advance the projects he initiated and to ensure that the seeds that he sowed in Bosnia and Herzegovina continue to grow and blossom.

For further information on the charity please contact:
info@helperscharity.com
Website: www.helperscharity.com

5

Damien Richardson

Damien Richardson is a happily married family man with seven children and another on the way. However, life was not always this good for him. At a young age he tried out and became addicted to heroin and other drugs. His father asked every person he met to pray for his son and his unfaltering faith was paramount in Damien arriving in the village of Medjugorje for the first time back in 1996. Damien's visit to the village was the first step on his long road to recovery. While in Medjugorje he visited the Cenacolo community and subsequently joined the house in Knock some years later.

This is Damien's testimony.

I was born to a good family in North Dublin. I had one older brother and one younger sister. When I was growing up, I was a very shy young fella and I wasn't very academic or anything like that but I was a happy-go-lucky lad.

I moved out of my parent's home when I was thirteen and moved into my grandmother's house. I went to a new school and met new people. When I was about fifteen years old, I started drinking and smoking hash. Everyone around me was doing it.

When I was about seventeen years old I went to a rave party and took an ecstasy tablet. I thought this was great and I was jumping around like a lunatic for the weekend. I thought this was what life is all about. It gave me confidence and I was able to talk to people.

I started taking ecstasy tablets every weekend and it was great but during the week I became very depressed. I was asking myself, 'What is this feeling I have never had before?' I thought that the reason I was feeling this way was because I didn't have these tablets inside me. So I kept taking the ecstasy tablets and so I kept feeling more down.

I was doing this for about six months and then one night after a rave, both me and a few friends had a smoke of heroin. This had the opposite effect of ecstasy and instead of jumping around it made me slow down. I was smoking it for a while and it got to a stage that it wasn't really affecting me anymore and so it escalated then to using a needle.

My life totally changed and I became a different person. I did a lot of stuff that you wouldn't normally do and I regret a lot of it. That was the life I was leading for a good few years. I was in trouble with the police a few times and I ended up in prison.

My dad was always a great man for praying and he had every person he met praying for me at that time. It was later that I understood the meaning of the power of prayer.

He was shown a video about two American girls who had been to Medjugorje. The girls had been speaking about how they had been addicted to drugs. They went to Medjugorje and were now living good again. So my dad was thinking, 'Right! I have to get Damien to Medjugorje.' I was twenty-three at the time and although I was still on the drugs I wasn't as bad as I had been previously.

So he sort of tricked me into going. He showed me travel brochures of Croatia with beautiful beaches and scenic mountains and so I said I would go.

An hour before we boarded the plane I was smoking heroin at the back of the airport. I slept on the plane on the way over because I was so out of my head. I remember waking up on the bus on the way from Croatia to Medjugorje and seeing all these people around me praying the rosary and I thought to myself, 'What am I after getting myself into?'

When I arrived at the village in 1996 I sussed the place out for an hour or so and I decided that I wanted to go home. I was saying, 'I want my passport, I need to get out of here.'

I had lots of bad thoughts in my head and I couldn't sleep for three days because of the heat and the effects of the drugs.

On the fourth morning I woke up after getting a few hours of sleep on a bench beside the statue of Our Lady in the grounds of St James Church. I stood there and I just felt this peace in my heart that I had never had before.

It was pure peace and serenity. The sun was shining on my face and it was a beautiful moment. I felt that God was real and Our Lady was real and everything began to make sense to me.

I began hanging around with a group of young people and they brought me to confession. Some of them would have been involved with Youth 2000 and other prayer groups. I was amazed at these young people who weren't afraid to pray or walk down the road with rosary beads dangling out of their hands.

I was due to go home after the first week but the tour operator came to our house one day and said the flights were overbooked due to the fact that the Irish Guards, who had been helping out in Bosnia after the war, needed to get home. They offered us to stay for an extra week, fully paid for with some spending money, so naturally I was delighted.

I also went up that week to visit the Cenacolo community for the first time. Community Cenacolo was set up by an Italian nun called Sr Elvira in 1983 in Saluzzo in northern Italy, for both men and women. She had a desire to work with people who had addictions. The first house was in Italy and there are over sixty houses around the world today. One of the main Cenacolo houses is in Medjugorje. When I visited the house I felt that the lads that were there were all so happy. There was something in their eyes. They didn't look like drug addicts. After my first trip to Medjugorje had ended, I went home and back to my girlfriend Mary, who was also a heroin addict and who I had been going out with for about a year before.

I was still on the drugs but something had changed inside me and there were a lot of things that I wouldn't do like before. I had a lot of difficulties, but eventually I went on a methadone programme for six years.

In that time, Mary and I had our first child. She was born a methadone baby and was very sick in hospital for a few weeks.

We went back to Medjugorje as a couple and with our first born a few times. We were still on drugs and methadone but I still went back. When I was in moments of despair, it was like recharging the batteries for me.

In 2002 I felt suicidal. It was like I was in a black hole and someone was putting their hands on my head and pushing me deeper into the black hole. I was in so much pain that I felt the only answer would be for me to kill myself.

I rang my mother and I broke down telling her I couldn't do this anymore. Within three days, my sister was bringing me over to Medjugorje again.

After a few days there, once again, I went up to the community Cenacolo house and was talking to one of the lads there. He told me that the drugs were not the problem, that the drugs would always be there. He told me that I had to change my life. In that moment, I felt like it was God speaking to me and I knew he was right. He told me that they had recently opened a community Cenacolo in Ireland, in Knock, Co. Mayo.

I asked him what I needed to do to get in there and he told me that I needed to attend a few meetings first. When I got home to Dublin, the first thing I did was ring Cenacolo in Knock.

I said, 'I'm a drug addict and I need help.'

They told me that I had to be off all the methadone and drugs before they would take me in. So I went to my doctor and told him that I wanted to come off the methadone.

I knew I needed to do a quick detox to get into the place in Knock.

I moved back to my dad's house and began the detox. I was on different tablets to help me cope with the effects. It took four weeks and the pain was excruciating. It was the worst month of my life.

I had this determination inside me and if I was going to die doing it then that was OK because I couldn't go on living with drugs anymore.

So I finished the detox and continued with the meetings and eventually went down to Knock. I stayed in a B & B first for eight days and eventually moved into the house.

When I got into Cenacolo in Knock there was no radio, no television, no newspapers or internet and no smoking allowed. It was very hard for a drug addict because there was no escape. I couldn't just go off and switch on the television or anything like that.

I was given a 'guardian angel' who was a guy who had been in the programme for a couple of months. He would stay by my side for the first two months. He slept on the bottom bunk underneath me. If I went to the toilet, he was standing outside the door waiting. It was very annoying especially because drug addicts like to be on their own, hiding away from the world. It was very hard to get used to and for the first few weeks I didn't speak to anyone. I was very down in myself.

I began praying the rosary and we had adoration every day. I felt that this prayer thing was actually working and it was the first time I was really praying from the heart.

Community Cenacolo operates through the Divine Providence. There is no paid staff and there is no charge for the programme – it's completely free. They get no government funding and so depend on the generosity of people.

If you haven't got something, you pray for it. People arrive at the house with donations of food and clothes and it is here that you really see God working.

The daily routine meant that we got up at six in the morning and had a wash. We then went into the chapel, opened the tabernacle and started praying the first joyful mystery. After this, we would do a Bible reading of the day and then we would talk about how we were feeling over the past few days.

At 8 a.m. we would go in for breakfast and at 8.30 a.m. work would start. There could be two people looking after the animals on the farm; someone else working in the kitchen and two others in the workshop cutting the wood for the fire and working in the vegetable garden. Other times people would be assigned to building work and cleaning work.

At 12 o'clock we would finish up and go in for lunch and then we would have some free time for about half an hour. Sometimes I would play football or other times do my washing. There were no washing machines so we had to wash our own clothes by hand.

We would pray the sorrowful mysteries and work until 5 o'clock, then we would go back into the chapel and be out in time for dinner at 6.30 p.m. After dinner we had a bit of free time and it was normal for people to go for a walk, especially with someone in there that they might not have been getting on with. We would talk about our difficulties and encourage each other and then we would retire at 9 p.m.

I was in Community Cenacolo in Knock, Co. Mayo, for a year and then I was transferred to the Cenacolo house in Medjugorje. They don't keep you in the one house all the time so you are moved around and meet addicts from all different countries.

Cenacolo was just what I needed – prayer, friendship and hard work. When I left the community and came home to Dublin, I felt that God had given me my life back and the first thing I wanted to do was get married. That is exactly what we did in 2005.

For our honeymoon, we went to Dubrovnik for three days and then on to the village of Medjugorje for the rest of the honeymoon to say thanks to Our Lady Queen of Peace for all the help she had given us.

Also during this time, I joined the Legion of Mary and I am still a member to this day. I do voluntary work in the Morning Star men's homeless hostel. I meet a lot of addicts and offer support and tell them about Community Cenacolo.

To date, my wife and I are off drugs ten years thanks to God and his holy mother. We have six children of our own now, one foster child and another baby on the way.

We pray the rosary with the kids every night, go to Mass together and try to encourage them in the Catholic faith.

I haven't missed the rosary in ten years, since the day I walked into Cenacolo. In a way, I'm afraid to miss it because I never want to go back to that dark place I was in when there were drugs in my life.

Another significant part of my own personal journey was that I started my own waste disposal business. A few years ago, I was called out to clear rubbish from the house of an old lady who had died. As I was moving the rubbish I found this old book called *Our Martyrs*.

It was written in 1896 by a priest called Fr Denis Murphy SJ. It is a record of those who suffered death for the Catholic faith under the Penal Laws in Ireland. The penalty for being discovered attending Mass was death. Most of them were hung, drawn and quartered. Men, women and children were put in chains and sent as slaves to the West Indies and the Caribbean Islands because they wouldn't renounce their Catholic faith.

I just felt that people needed to read this book and see how past generations suffered to give us the freedom to partake in the sacraments that we have today. I managed to get the book republished so it is in print today.

I don't earn any money from it. A priest friend of mine, Fr Michael Ross SDB, is the treasurer and looks after it and we distribute the books to priests and lay people.

What does Medjugorje mean to me?

I think that over in Medjugorje Our Lady just gently takes you by the hand and leads you to her son Jesus. The Medjugorje experience is indescribable.

There is also the social aspect of Medjugorje which is extremely important because you get to meet and bond with so many people and hear their stories. There is definitely something real out there and I really feel I would be still on drugs or dead only for Medjugorje.

God has been very good to me and my family. I thank God and Our Lady of Medjugorje, Queen of Peace, for these blessings every day.

For more information on the Community Cenacolo in Knock please visit the website at www.cenacolocommunityireland.ie or telephone 00353 94 9388286.

6

Maureen Maher

Maureen Maher brought the first group of Irish pilgrims out to Medjugorje back in the early eighties. When her youngest daughter was born with Down's syndrome, she was searching for answers as to why her baby wasn't 'normal' like her other children. Being present during an apparition and subsequent experiences in the village helped her come to terms with her daughter Nicky's disability and subsequent death.

This is Maureen's testimony.

When my youngest daughter, Nicky, was born with Down's syndrome back in 1981, I was extremely upset and struggled to come to terms with her disability. I was so afraid for her future as I was very naïve and knew nothing about the condition.

I picked up the newspaper one day and read that the mother of God was appearing in a small remote village in Medjugorje to six young children. I instantly believed that it was real and that she was appearing and I felt drawn to bring a group over to the village.

I approached the local priest in the parish at the time and I was simply flabbergasted when he said it was no problem and that I would have his support. So, myself and another lady from Galway brought out the first group of Irish pilgrims to Medjugorje. I brought my daughter Nicky with me as a two-year-old in her buggy and I was hoping for a miracle.

When we arrived at the airport, I was so excited after organising the group of eager pilgrims. Although I was Irish, I was also an American citizen and held an American passport. I was told that I couldn't travel as I would need a special visa to get into Yugoslavia, as it was called at the time.

Nicky was sitting in the buggy and the rest of my family were also in the airport seeing me off. They were so happy that I was going to this special place. I was devastated when I heard I couldn't travel that day. However, I was determined that I was going to get there. It was a bank holiday weekend and as I waved the pilgrims off, I set about getting the necessary documentation together. The priest had a friend who was a

Garda and along with another friend of mine, they pulled together and I was able to get an emergency Irish passport.

I travelled via London a few days later and when I arrived there, it was just such a joy. I got a huge welcome from the pilgrims and also from the local people, whose house we were staying in.

Medjugorje was a very poor farming village and so it was normal to stay in the villagers' homes as there were no hotels at the time. There would be one shower between the group and the rooms were basic but very clean. The host families opened their hearts to the pilgrims and they lived by the earth. You might see chickens running around during the day and that would be your dinner that evening.

No one minded this basic sort of living and the hospitable host families were so grateful to the pilgrims that they always went out of their way to make our stay comfortable.

In return, we usually left them some clothing and also did a collection at the end of the trip which we presented to them before we went home.

Back then, in the early eighties, the apparitions took place in the priest's house, about fifty yards from St James Church. People would gather outside and listen to the chirping of the birds, waiting patiently for the apparition to take place.

There were priests and some sick people allowed in, to be present in the small room where the six young people were having their apparition in the evening.

I was waiting outside with many others when Fr Slavko, who was the visionaries' spiritual director, ushered me in with my daughter who was sitting in her buggy.

The visionaries started praying the rosary and so did everyone else in the room.

I remember seeing one of the visionaries getting a bit distracted during prayer and I thought this was quite normal as it is easy to get distracted in everyday life.

They continued on praying the rosary and in the middle of prayer, in one swift movement, the six children were down on their knees at the one time. Their eyes were looking up and they were transfixed on one solitary spot. Their lips were moving, like they were talking, but there was no sound to be heard.

I saw nothing but I could feel a presence in the room. I was very conscious that Nicky was there with me and I kept praying and asking Our Lady to heal her. I was hoping a miracle would happen.

The apparition lasted about ten minutes and then they all raised their heads higher and seemed to watch Our Lady ascend into heaven and then they all made the sign of the cross. It seemed so very normal for them and I didn't feel like there was anything false about it all.

The miraculous thing was that they were speaking to Our Lady but nobody in the room could hear them. It was like a private conversation between them and Our Lady.

I was so moved and I felt something in my heart saying to me that this child was a gift from God, just like all my other children and that there was a place on this earth for everyone. I felt I must love her and cherish her and all will be well. The peace and acceptance I felt was overwhelming.

When I was in the room, I remember seeing a priest who was very emotional during the apparition and when we got outside we both shared our stories with each other. He told me that he had been having doubts about his vocation but now felt that he understood what a wonderful gift priesthood was and that was why he had been overcome by emotion.

From that day on, I felt totally different and accepting of my daughter. Before that, I would find that I would want her one day and not want her the next. I just wanted her to be 'normal' like the rest of my children. I seriously worried about how I would cope and what the future held.

That all left me and I knew everything was going to be just fine.

In thanksgiving, I decided that I was going to continue bringing groups out to Medjugorje and that is what I am still doing today, almost thirty years later.

One time, during one of my many trips out to Medjugorje, I was standing outside St James Church and there were many people around me all looking up at the sun. I felt that I couldn't look because I thought the bright light would be blinding but I still felt drawn to look.

I saw the sun zooming in and out and spinning. It looked like the white host with IHS in the middle of it in big letters. I saw a figure with its arms around the host but I couldn't see a face. Gold stars started to appear in the sky and it was like I was in a beautiful big park. I then saw a huge cross which seemed to take up the whole sky. This disappeared and I saw a figure who I took to be Padre Pio, and a baby was floating in the sky. Lights seemed to be flickering on and off and I was down on my knees and knew it was something supernatural that was happening. I was aware of everything going on around me.

I then saw what I at first thought was a bird, but then it seemed to transform into the figure of Our Lady and she was coming towards me. It was all happening very quickly and she was smiling and I felt this tremendous peace surround me. I desperately wanted to see more but it all disappeared and I went into the church.

Sometimes, we were told that Our Lady was going to appear on Apparition Hill at night time and the visionaries would invite the pilgrims to come up. We would climb the rocky mountain with our torches and there would be music and song and prayer.

On one such occasion, after an apparition, they translated into English what the visionaries had to say.

They described how Our Lady came in a beautiful light with two angels by her side. She extended her hands out over the gathered crowd and looked at everyone there. They said she offered everything that was in the people's hearts up to her son Jesus and that she would specially recommend all the sick to her son. She then gave everyone her motherly blessing.

I also went out towards the end of the Bosnian War and I brought my eldest daughter, Suzanne, over with me. They desperately needed aid and so I rang Dunnes Stores and they gave me brand new clothes – underwear and children's clothes – to bring over to the families and orphans. My friend's husband was a dentist and he gave me toothbrushes and toothpaste and my own doctor gave me antibiotics to bring over.

We also fundraised for those who had lost their husbands during the war and for the orphaned children. It was truly emotional seeing the pain and suffering the people had been through. I remember still, hearing bombs in the distance.

Our Lady had told the visionaries that Medjugorje would never be touched during the war. It was said that a war pilot had tried to bomb the village but a great cloud had come over as he was targeting and he aborted his plan.

The communist army were sent in at the beginning of the war and told to stop this 'revolution' that was happening in the village. The soldiers reported back to their superior's weeks later saying: 'There is no revolution going on here – these people are simply praying.'

I also saw lots of physical and spiritual healing during my time in Medjugorje. Only a few years ago, I witnessed an American woman who was in a wheelchair at Mass one day. During the healing prayers, she felt like she wanted to get up and stand. Her husband was pushing her down saying, 'No, you can't, you will hurt yourself.' But she kept saying that she felt a heat in her legs and wanted to stand. She got up out of the wheelchair and walked home.

There was also another lady who was blind and during the consecration in Mass, she told how she could see the white vestments and the host and then she was able to see everything fully. Her daughter was with her and she saw her for the first time. It was very emotional.

On another trip, I was sitting up at the Blue Cross at the base of Apparition Hill praying. There was a little white handkerchief dangling from the statue. There wasn't a breath of air and all was still but I thought I saw it move. Then I saw a vision of Our Lady but she was crying. I didn't know why she was crying but tears began flowing from my eyes and I couldn't stop. Then many miniature priests, cardinals and bishops appeared around her but she was still crying. I never really understood what it was all about but years later when the scandal broke about priests abusing children, I realised the significance of what I saw.

My daughter Nicky passed away very suddenly in 2008 at the tender age of twenty-six. She was a huge part of our life and, as a family, we were all devastated. Nicky had grown up to be a loving, independent and carefree spirit as she progressed through life.

At first I wasn't sure that I could go back to Medjugorje for some time but I had already made plans before she passed away to bring a group out that year.

I made the decision to go back in thanksgiving for her life and for all the graces and blessings I had received while she was on the earth. Mirjana, one of the visionaries, had prayed with Nicky when she was a toddler and had told me to pray over Nicky too.

It was emotional going back but I had realised what a gift Nicky was and how she enriched our lives and touched so many other people's lives. I felt her presence while I was there and felt she was not only there with Our Lady, but that she was beside me too.

What does Medjugorje mean to me?

Medjugorje to me is an oasis of peace. It is a place where there are great graces and blessings in abundance if your heart and soul is open. You don't have to do anything when you are there – it just happens to you. You have to go to experience it for yourself.

I do believe it will be sanctioned by Rome eventually. The focus over there is on the sacraments, not the visionaries. It is about the Eucharist, the Mass, reconciliation, peace and love.

I saw the visionaries as young children and I see them today as grown adults with children of their own and I truly believe in the whole phenomenon that is Medjugorje.

Medjugorje has given me an inner peace and helped me cope with the grief after Nicky passed away as I know there is life after death and I know that she journeyed on from this life into a beautiful place.

For me, it is a foretaste of heaven.

7

Una Kenealy

Una Kenealy was instantly intrigued when she heard about the alleged appari-
tions back in the early eighties. After buying a pair of rosary beads in a religious
shop in Dublin she brought them over to the village and something inexplicable
happened to the silver beads. Una also witnessed a most beautiful event up on
the small mountain Podbrdo one night as the visionaries had an apparition.
   This is Una's testimony.

The first time I heard about Medjugorje was on the radio back in the
early eighties. Straightaway I thought I would just love to go there.
Although I had not heard the full story, I believed in it immediately. A
few months later, I was coming out of church after Sunday Mass, when
I saw a lady talking to a few people about taking a group to Medjugorje
in May or June of 1983. The lady's name was Maureen Maher.

My own mother also showed a big interest in going so she went with
Maureen and a group from Beaumont in 1983. She loved every minute
of it.

The following year, 1984, in June, I travelled with Maureen and an
even bigger group for my first visit to Medjugorje. It had such an impact
on me that I decided to bring the eldest of my three daughters, who was
then eight years old, with me the following year, and this I did.

A year or two later in October I brought out my twin daughters, who
were nearly eight years old. We travelled with another friend, Phyllis,
who was on her thirteenth visit.

It was on this trip that we had a wonderful experience – one we
would never, ever forget. In those days Our Lady was appearing every
evening up at the back of the choir area in the church. People would be
outside waiting for her to appear at the usual time of 6.40 p.m.

There were many tall trees outside the church and you could hear
the birds rushing from one tree to another. It was quite noisy as they
chirped away and rustled amidst the leaves. The moment Our Lady
appeared, you would know, because there was complete silence. The
birds would suddenly stop chirping. Once Our Lady had gone, they
would be back making noise again.

After Mass one evening and after the daily apparition of Our Lady to the visionaries in the church, my friend Phyllis told me she had just heard that Our Lady was to appear to the visionaries on the small mountain Podbrdo at 10 p.m. that same night. I was told to keep this information to myself (for safety reasons) as they didn't want too many people going up to the mountain at night.

We dashed home for dinner, got ready and hopped into a taxi which took us to the base of Podbrdo. Phyllis was a bit quicker on her feet than me so she took one of my daughters with her. They climbed to the cross halfway up the mountain and knelt down very close to the visionaries. By the time I got up the mountain with my other twin, there must have been about three hundred people there which meant we had to go up higher than anybody else and stay at the edge of the crowd. So we ended up facing the big mountain (Križevac) and St James Church, which we could see in the distance.

We had noticed earlier that night when en route to the small mountain, that the sky was dotted with small stars, but only in the Medjugorje area. Up on the mountain, everyone was praying out loud and then there was silence. We knew that the visionaries were seeing and speaking with Our Lady.

At this point, miniature gold stars began to fall all around us. They were the size you would find on a child's school copy. Everyone's head was nodding as we watched the stars fall. They seemed to vanish just before hitting the ground. At the time I never thought to put my hand out to catch one.

Suddenly a castle appeared on the big mountain. It was a dull grey colour and looked like an eastern style structure. There had been dreadful thunder and lightning the night before and I remember one woman being terrified in her room thinking it was the end of the world.

As we stood on the mountain we could see the thunder and lightning had moved to the valley behind the big mountain. Every time the lightning lit up the sky the castle appeared on the mountain in front of us. Every time the lightning went, the castle went. This happened about six or seven times.

An American man standing beside me said, 'Look, look, the house of the Lord.' My daughter pulled at my jacket saying, 'Mammy, look.' I personally didn't feel it was a good sign because it was so grey. I would have expected the house of Our Lord to be white or gold. I didn't think much more about it and went home to bed.

The next morning, my friend Phyllis was up early as she climbed the big mountain most mornings before breakfast. She was passing one of the visionaries' house (I think it may have been Ivan's), where he was talking to a group about the apparition the night before.

He said it was normal for Our Lady to appear in a grey or blue gown but the previous night Our Lady had appeared in white and gold. She appeared with a host of angels and they were covered in stardust! I remember thinking: 'Wow! That was the stardust that fell on top of us. We were truly blessed.'

The reason Our Lady was all dressed in white and gold was because it was the 70th anniversary of the last apparition of Fatima when the Miracle of the Sun took place. On 13 October 1917, the sun came close, went back and changed colour and danced. It could be seen for many miles and was witnessed by thousands of people.

One year after our lovely experience on the little mountain, Podbrdo, I found myself back in Medjugorje. A lady approached me, a complete stranger, but she recognised me from the previous trip. She said, 'You were here last year. Were you on the big mountain that night?'

I said, 'No, I was on the small mountain'.

She said, 'Could you see the castle?'

I said, 'Yes.'

She continued to tell me the castle appeared on the big mountain right beside her about six or seven times.

Sometime later, a priest from Medjugorje was in Ireland. He was giving a talk on Medjugorje on the Navan Road in Dublin. I went along with my friend Maureen. After the talk, we went to a local priest's house for a cup of tea. While there, another priest arrived.

Maureen suggested I tell the priest what I saw on the mountain in Medjugorje. When I told him about the castle appearing he said, 'Well you know when Lourdes or Fatima or both was going on there were numerous reports of a castle in the sky.' He said it was supposedly the devil trying to interrupt the people praying while Our Lady was appearing. After seeing the grey castle, this I could believe!

On another of my trips to Medjugorje I had another special experience. One day I was sitting in the sunshine outside St James Church. Being lunchtime, there were very few people around. I was quietly praying and trying to take in the wonderfulness of the daily happenings (apparitions, conversions, cures, sightings, etc.) in this small village of Medjugorje.

I was so thankful that I was alive and living in the right century, the right time, so as to visit and experience the reality surrounding Medjugorje. When, suddenly, a young girl ran down the steps of the church shouting, 'Mammy, look, look!' The young girl was about seven or eight years of age. She was from somewhere in the UK. She had a pair of rosary beads in her hand. She was telling her mother that her silver beads had turned gold.

I felt so moved by this and thought what a beautiful gift from Our Lady for this little girl to cherish forever.

Knowing that there was a good chance I would return to Medjugorje the following year, I decided to look for silver rosary beads when I got back to Dublin, to have ready for my next visit.

Five months later, in November, while in Dublin city shopping I came across a religious shop on Clarendon Street lane, near the church. At the back of the shop, in a shoe box, were some little white plastic boxes and inside each of them was a set of silver rosary beads. The chains were silver and the ball-shaped beads were of the cheapest silver colour. I bought four pairs. One for myself and one for each of my three girls. I slept with my set of silver beads under my pillow from the November until going to Medjugorje the following June. Some nights I said prayers with them, but never the full rosary.

When June came the following year, I brought the silver beads with me to Medjugorje together with the three white boxes containing the silver beads belonging to my daughters.

These three sets were never used and were still the same as the day I had bought them – cheap silver. I really wanted to get all the four sets blessed on this trip and I used my own beads all the time I was there.

Halfway through the week-long pilgrimage, I went into confession and when I came out I sat on a bench in the grounds of the church. My cousin, who was with me on the trip, turned to me and said that she thought the links between her husband's black beads had turned from silver to gold.

I looked down at my beads only to find that they had turned a murky kind of gold colour. For some reason one bead remained silver, but you could see it was slowly changing.

When I returned home I took my beads out of my bag to show my family. They were now a shiny gold colour. When I opened the other three sets, I could see that they too had changed but were a duller shade than mine and still are to this day. I truly cherish this wonderful keepsake and feel that the beads belonging to my three girls haven't reached that shiny gold colour yet because they are not used enough.

I hope and pray that some day their beads will be as gold as mine. Even though I don't pray with my beads as often as I should, they still seem to be a deeper shade of gold each time I look at them. They mean so much to me.

I know, as a mother, that if I was lucky enough to get to heaven and there was any way I could help my children, my friends and my family from above then I would.

So it is very natural to me that Our Lady is appearing and asking us to pray and telling us how we should live good lives. It makes perfect sense to me that Our Lady, our Mother, would come with messages and guidance to help us, her children here on earth. That is what she did in Lourdes and Fatima.

What does Medjugorje mean to me?

To me, when you are in Medjugorje, the air you breathe seems like it is filled with so much holiness.

You can find a quiet spot, maybe a rock on the little mountain to sit on and lose yourself while praying, yet feeling that you are not alone.

You feel Jesus, Mary and the angels, even your loved ones in heaven are not just close but actually beside you.

When I think of Medjugorje I get a lump in my throat.

To me, it is the nearest place to heaven on this earth.

8

Stuart McGovern

When Stuart McGovern visited Medjugorje at twelve years of age he saw a piece of heaven in the clouds. However, tragic events in his life meant he turned his back on God for a while. Returning to the village as an adult many years later, Stuart rediscovered the sense of peace in his heart that he had experienced years earlier and his spiritual life and love for God was reinstated.

This is Stuart's testimony.

I wasn't quite sure what was going on as I looked up at the face of Ivan Dragicevic when I was twelve years old. I was kneeling beside him and the five other visionaries of Medjugorje on Podbrdo, or Apparition Hill, just three years after the apparitions had begun. I knew it was a solemn moment, and I knew that Our Lady was appearing, but I had expected a bit more. I looked at Ivan's face as he spoke, but I couldn't hear anything. Then it was all over.

My mother had gone to Medjugorje a year earlier and had experienced a conversion. She had witnessed a miracle while she was there, as had the rest of her small group, and she had come home a different person. They were all convinced that Medjugorje was a place of special graces. Her real wish was to get the whole family back there, especially my father, to share in the excitement of it all. Twelve months later she got her wish. It took us two days to get there and we only stayed for three days, but for me, they were to prove to be three very special days.

As I descended Apparition Hill that night, I ran ahead of the family as a normal twelve year old likes to do. It was a bright night and it was easy enough to see the small, narrow track down the side of the hill. When I got about halfway down I stopped to wait for the others. As I let the other pilgrims pass me by I looked up at the night sky. I wasn't quite prepared for the scene that appeared before my eyes. Within the clouds I saw Jesus on the cross. His features were very distinct and I watched as time seemed to stand still. I looked away and looked back and he was still there. It struck me so much how similar the picture I was looking at was with the picture in my Bible at home. I said nothing to anyone. That was my little secret that I wasn't prepared to share for the time being. Would anyone even believe me anyway? Jesus on the cross – what did it mean?

Three years later my father was diagnosed with cancer and was given three months to live. My world fell apart and I didn't know what to do about it. I was fifteen years old and certainly wasn't ready for this. We prayed for a healing and my mother had half the country praying for him as well. It wasn't to be though, and although he got his wish to make it until Christmas Day, he died that evening. My mother was forty-two years old and had four young children left to look after, ranging in age from five to seventeen.

I blamed God for it all. After all that prayer surely he should have healed my dad, especially since he was so young and he had four children to look after. What kind of a God wouldn't hear those prayers? I spent the next number of years very angry and very unhappy. I didn't want to know God and didn't want him in my life if that was the way he was going to be with those he apparently loved.

Suddenly, there was a massive void in my life. The two I called 'father' were somehow gone and I was left to cope with it all alone. Things weren't too bad when I was out of the house and I could manage to distract myself enough, but being at home was a trigger for all my anger and my poor mother bore the brunt of it.

I went back to Medjugorje a year later with a group of young people, but my heart wasn't in it and I got more of a kick out of being in the pub than in the church. The minimum drinking age was sixteen in the former Yugoslavia so we spent night after night in the pub. This was to become somewhat of a pattern for the next decade of my life.

Consequently I drifted further away from the Church and from any kind of relationship with Jesus Christ. In my twenties I was involved in a pretty active social scene. Life was great apart from the unease in my soul that occasionally caused me to reflect on the existence of God. This was something I never stopped believing, that God existed. I never doubted it even when I refused to acknowledge him or have him in my life in any way. I always believed in Jesus Christ; sure hadn't I seen him in Medjugorje.

In 1995 I qualified as an engineer and that same year I took off to Australia where I stayed until 1997. When I returned home I managed to get a job with a large mobile phone company as a telecoms engineer and spent the next four or five years travelling the world with them. I enjoyed this immensely but there was a niggling feeling that I wanted to do more with my life. I was feeling a draw to a simpler life but I fought it tooth and nail because I was enjoying things as they were.

I had a good job, a girlfriend of three years and was on the verge of buying a house when things took a dramatic change of direction. In the space of a week I broke up with my girlfriend and left the job. It was a turning point in my life and I had no idea where it would take me, but after a lot of discernment I realised that it was something that had to be done. I had been spending a bit more time in prayer and popping into Mass a bit during the week. I was slowly forgiving the Lord for what he had done to me thirteen years previously when he snatched my father from me. I was starting to realise that I needed the Lord in my life for my own personal happiness and peace, something that had been noticeably missing over the previous years. My memory of Medjugorje was buried somewhere deep within me so as not to interfere with my active social life, but now it was starting to surface again, and now I felt I was ready to start a new life, somewhat reconciled with God.

I was drawn more and more to daily Mass and adoration in my local church and I was beginning to enjoy sitting in the quietness. After a couple of years I found a nice little place to rent on Paddock hill in Glendalough, Co. Wicklow. It was only a room, but it was all I needed and it looked out over the hills. I was to spend almost seven years there in all, a great opportunity to soak in the silence of the countryside and enjoy the beauty of nature which is so prominent in that place.

I started a small painting and decorating business where I just worked for myself. It suited me down to the ground and it was a welcome change after years of sitting in front of a computer.

However, while I slowly came to terms with the changes that were taking place in my life, I came to understand the importance of coming to terms with myself. The silence of that place was the means for much inner work that was needed, a letting go and an acceptance of all that had happened in my life, and of course the acknowledgement of the anger and grief that I had been carrying around with me for so many years.

Shortly after moving to the hills of Glendalough I decided I would return to Medjugorje. One of my memories of the place was climbing Cross Mountain with my father. I longed to go back to see how it had all changed and perhaps to be present at another apparition. I booked to go with my cousin so that I would be there for my 33rd birthday.

And so it was that in July 2006 I finally returned after almost seventeen years. I realised after the week that I wouldn't be able to stay away for that long again. It was like stepping out of the world and into an oasis of peace. Many will say that the most striking thing about Medjugorje is the sense of peace, and it was that peace that had me already planning my next trip.

When I got home I put it to my two brothers. We went over in September for four days and had a few days in Dubrovnik by the beach to follow, but before I left Medjugorje for Dubrovnik I had changed my return flight. I left my brothers in Dubrovnik and went back to Medjugorje for another week alone. I never saw the sun spinning or any other unusual events that many say they see, but I had found a peace that I knew I had been seeking for a long time. During that week I met a young priest who has become a good friend and through him I have met so many young people who are also seeking a life with the peace of knowing and believing in God and having the comfort of Our Lady as a Mother.

In the following years I returned to Medjugorje several times. Mostly I went with small groups or alone and once only with an organised pilgrimage. Each time was different and each experience served to increase my faith and give me strength to try to remain faithful to the Church and to the teachings of the gospel. While I still struggled with the world and all it offered, I found myself being drawn more into prayer and the sacraments and a desire to know more about the scriptures. I was beginning to realise that prayer, primarily the Mass but also Eucharistic Adoration, the rosary and Divine Mercy Chaplet were the means of growing in my relationship with God. For me, this was where life made sense, spending time daily with God. Medjugorje was certainly the catalyst for my personal relationship with Jesus Christ and his Mother. Daily Mass and other forms of prayer were what sustained it.

In the following years I 'accidentally' got involved in bringing groups out to Medjugorje. I had decided to go with a few friends for Easter 2009. It was to be just the four of us, but we decided to mention it to a few others and see if anyone else might like to join us. Sure enough people were interested and the fact that we were organising it independently of the big operators meant it was far less expensive. There were a few families with young children and plenty of teachers who were on holidays for Easter. All in all we made up a group of fifty, ranging from two to forty-five years old. However, the bulk of the group were in their twenties. I was amazed at the interest in the trip and while it was a bit of hassle to organise, it was a joy to see a group of young people so enthusiastic about a pilgrimage to Medjugorje.

One of my great memories of that trip was on the plane on the way home. A group of girls who were on the trip with us were entertaining half the plane, and as I watched them laughing and joking I wondered what the rest of the people coming home from Zadar must have thought. Ireland was in a depression and here's a bunch of young people so full of life and joy.

The following Easter we decided to do the same again. This time there were many from the previous year but also some new people and again the number reached about fifty. Each day we would organise one activity for those in the group who wanted to take part in it and then the rest of the day was free for private time or whatever people wanted to do. This maintained a good group spirit and also gave people a chance to have their own personal space. I always feel that a visit up Apparition Hill or Cross Mountain alone or with one other is a great chance to take time out from the world and have some much needed silence and reflection.

We returned in similar style for the third year in Easter 2011; again, around fifty young people going in search of something that the world just couldn't fulfil in their lives. Again I had the privilege of organising the trip and again we were blessed to have a great young priest with us who had obliged us the previous two years also.

As I spoke to the different people on the three different pilgrimages, there seemed to be a common thread running through the lives of each one. Few were on a mission to try and save the world or were full of ambition to be big success stories. They all seemed to be content with their lives and had a kind of acceptance of the way things were, while also desiring to fulfil the mission that God had for them. This was not to say that their lives were devoid of problems and issues that were causing them difficulties, but I think their faith was enabling them to accept certain things that they could do very little about and trust that God had a plan and that he was on their side. It was a bit like the trust a small child has in a father who is looking after things.

The messages of Medjugorje, when we read them down through the years, have a common theme: to pray and to keep praying with the Eucharist at the forefront of our lives. During the times in my life that I try to live these messages I find I get strength and a conviction that can easily go astray when I take my focus off the Lord. A bit like Peter who had great faith to step out of the boat and walk on the water, but then took his eyes off Jesus and started to sink. I can safely say that I have lived that piece of scripture over and over.

I often wonder about the happenings in Medjugorje. I wonder why Our Lady has come for so long and what the reason for her coming is. God must have a very good reason for letting her come every day for thirty or so years, and yet she seems to be saying the same thing to us over and over. The more I read the messages the more I realise that Our Lady is calling for us to have faith in her son and to live that faith, and that prayer is the means to grow strong in our faith.

To go there is to experience a place that is different from anywhere else in the world. To come home and live the message is another story altogether. Fr Svet often says at his talks that the pilgrimage starts the moment we step off the plane after returning home from Medjugorje and I have to agree with him. It's pretty easy to pray, to go to Mass and to pray the rosary in Medjugorje. It's coming home and putting into practice all the things that are asked of us by Our Lady – allowing God to take first place in everything in our daily lives – that is the hard part.

While this sounds like something that could possibly make you miserable, in reality it has the opposite effect. Over the past twenty years I have experienced what it is like to live on both sides of the fence. My efforts to keep God out of my life only served to cause me to become more unhappy with my lot. As much as I searched in the world, I couldn't find what I thought would fulfil the longing in my heart. I had distracted myself as much as I could and finally reached a point where I needed to step back from my life for a moment and be a bit honest with myself. I was running away from the only One who could help me. I was afraid that if I started to turn to the Lord, he would ask too much of me. All the things that a Christian life demands were too frightening for me and I wasn't willing to go down that road just then. I thought that in time, when I was older and life was easier, I would be more responsible and would surely be more accepting of the demands that God would make on me. For now, things were too exciting and life was to be lived in the way I thought it should be lived. Such were my thoughts and my fears.

What I have come to learn on my journey of faith throughout my life – one that I would say began on that first trip to Medjugorje with the sowing of a very valuable seed of faith that was somewhat nurtured in the following years through prayer until the death of my father and that remained hidden and buried for so long after that – could probably be summed up in the words of St Augustine: 'Our hearts are restless until they rest in you, O Lord.'

Medjugorje helped me to recognise that truth. It allowed me to experience a long-awaited peace and it helped me to understand how to maintain that peace.

Another important thing that I have learned through my time in Medjugorje is that God actually has our best interests at heart. Of course life is difficult and things happen that we find very hard to understand, but his plan is an eternal one that involves eternal life with him in heaven, and for me that is most reassuring.

9

Derek Farrell

Derek Farrell was heartbroken when his fiancée broke up with him back in 1985. When his brother, who had Crohn's disease, bought him a ticket for Medjugorje, Derek didn't want to go. However, travelling over to Medjugorje the following year turned out to be the catalyst in meeting his future wife.

This is Derek's testimony.

My story starts on Halloween of October 1985, when I collected my then fiancée from work and she told me that she didn't want to marry me. We had been together for four and a half years and were due to be married on 6 June 1986. We had the church, the hotel, the wedding car, the photographer, the band – everything booked for the forthcoming wedding.

When she broke the devastating news to me that night, I felt so alone and afraid of the future. We had just bought a new house together and I had moved in on my own about three months previously. I was so looking forward to the following June when our wedding was supposed to take place.

When we broke up, I wanted to keep the house myself but I had no money to pay her the amount she was entitled to for her share.

I remember leaving my sister's house one evening and going home, crying myself to sleep with deep sadness and no hope for the future.

Family and friends started to give me money to pay my ex-fiancée off, but I said to them that I did not know when I would be able to pay them back. They all said not to worry about it, that I could pay them back in my own time.

At one stage, I had to stop people giving me money as I had too much! I paid it all back within eighteen months and ended up keeping the house, even though I couldn't see the point at that stage. I was so sad and lonely and I remember sitting at home in that lonely house one evening and saying to myself, 'I am a good person and I am finished with women!'

My brother, Joe, had been to Medjugorje in May 1985. He had Crohn's disease and had been very ill since he was fourteen years old. In 1985, he was 32.

He could not stop talking about Medjugorje when he came back and I was sick and tired of listening to him. In February of 1986, he told me that he had bought me a ticket and was bringing me to Medjugorje on 3 May that year. Immediately, I said, 'No way!' First of all, I didn't want to go to that place and, secondly, I told him that I would only go if I could pay for myself. However, my brother persisted and on 3 May 1986, we flew to Split with a group from Beaumont and we linked up with a group from Galway.

When we were on the coach travelling from the airport to the village of Medjugorje, I met a guy from Athlone and asked him what in the name of God was he doing going to Medjugorje.

He replied that his uncle, who was a priest, was meant to go but couldn't, so he was going for a sun tan instead. I told him that I heard there was a small town called Čitluk about 3 km away, where there were some bars that we could go into and have a few pints. It would be an escape from the 'holy place'; we never made it to Čitluk.

When we arrived at our house, there was one toilet between forty people. The food was awful and we were stuck with all these 'ol' ones' for the week. I kept thinking: 'God help us!'

I hated the first three days and asked my brother Joe how I could get out of there. He told me that there was only one bus and one plane per week and that I was stuck there whether I liked it or not.

After three days, I had confession with Fr Svet and it was as if he could see into my soul. I left confession with a sense that a heavy load had been lifted from my chest. I truly feel that Our Lady put her arms around me that day and has not let go of me since.

I felt hope, joy and peace in my heart and said to my brother and others in the group that we must tell people about this place when we get home.

So twelve of us got together on our return and put on a Medjugorje evening on 3 September 1986 in Beaumont Church. On the night, we showed a video of Medjugorje on a 50 ft screen. We invited speakers including Joe and Eleanor McFadden and Heather Parsons. The church held 800 but we had to borrow 600 more seats from the local school as the church was packed out for the evening.

I was doing MC for the night and there in the congregation was my future wife, Anne Moore. She had been to Dubrovnik in July of that year and went down to Medjugorje with her sister for a day and ended up spending five days in the village.

When she climbed Apparition Hill, she saw hundreds of crosses which people had left there from their pilgrimages. She was drawn to one brown wooden cross which our group leader had gotten made with all our names inscribed on it – all 120.

Out of the all those names Anne was drawn to one name – Derek Farrell – but she thought nothing of it at the time.

When we were advertising for the Medjugorje evening in Beaumont we had put up posters all over Dublin. Anne saw a poster in Rathmines Church and came along on the night with her sister and her dad.

When I was on the altar speaking, Anne turned around to her sister and said, 'That is the guy I am going to marry.'

We somehow met, in a group, shortly after that. I asked her out for a date and we had three dates over the next week and a half. On the third date, we both knew, and I asked her to marry me. She said, 'Yes.'

We travelled back to Medjugorje in May 1987 and decided to get engaged there. I didn't have an engagement ring so I gave her a rosary ring. We had a big party that night in the house where we were staying.

We married on 6 October 1987 and have three children: Simon, Chris and Hannah.

My brother, Joe, died of Crohn's disease in 1994 and I know he is enjoying his just reward with Our Lady in the highest part of heaven. Thanks, Joe, for bringing me to Medjugorje to Our Blessed Mother.

Our Lady Queen of Peace brought me to Medjugorje on 3 May 1986, wrapped her arms around me, and told me she loved me and that everything would be alright. She is still looking after me and my family ever since.

While I was in Medjugorje in 1986, Our Lady gave this powerful message on 8 May:

> Dear Children, You are the ones responsible for the messages. The source of grace is here, but you, dear children, are the vessels which transport the gifts. Therefore, dear children, I am calling you to do your job with responsibility. Each one shall be responsible according to his/her own ability. Dear children, I am calling you to give the gifts to others with love and not to keep them for yourselves. Thank you for having responded to my call.

10

Charlie Lennon

Charlie Lennon is a well-known traditional Irish musician. When his wife came home from a pilgrimage to Medjugorje, he noticed a 'change' in her and thought that he might go there one day. His subsequent visit to the village of Medjugorje prepared him for events that would happen in his life shortly after his return.

This is Charlie's testimony.

My first thoughts, when Medjugorje comes to mind, is of walking through its small fields on the way to Apparition Hill, absorbing the peace and quietness, the smell of the earth, the murmur of small groups in prayer. It brings me back to my childhood days and the simplicity of life in Ireland then.

As I make my way in my mind's eye to the foot of the hill, I picture the scene of the first appearance of Our Lady to the children some thirty years ago now, and wonder in awe at the fact that she is still coming to some of the visionaries to this very day.

I first became aware of the place when my wife Síle went there in the early nineties with a group from Dublin. We lived in Howth at the time and she was involved with prayer groups and was much more aware of happenings in Bosnia than I was. Of course, there was still fighting there at that time but that did not put her off going.

When she came back safe and well I could see a change in her. I couldn't put my finger on it but I was impressed and made a mental note that I should find out more about the place when I got time. Time was of course a difficulty and I was finding it hard to keep up with all that was going on in my life, juggling with work, home, music, as well as everyday family life.

Síle went again a couple of years later and, as I became more aware of what was happening there, I vowed to myself that I would go with her whenever the next opportunity arose. And it did, in 1998.

I was very impressed with the place and in particular with its people. They had a great devotion to Our Lord and to Our Lady. Every evening they came to St James Church to pray the full rosary and to participate in the Mass. On our first evening we went there in good time to discover that the church was overcrowded. I knelt down in the aisle but soon got a tap on the shoulder from a local woman many years my senior. She was offering me her seat. What hospitality! I thanked her, gracefully declined and moved aside to the crowded wall to reflect on her generosity.

The story of the large cross on the top of the nearby mountain fascinated me and brought home to me the faith and strength of character of the local people in the face of severe suppression.

We have gone back quite a number of times since then and I still feel the call to go. We live in Spiddal, Co. Galway now and five of us from the area went in 2005 with a group led by Eddie Stones and Fr Noel Burke. One elderly lady in our group had difficulty in walking. We were happy to see her able to walk to the church and back and around the shops. However, when she announced one day that she was going to climb Cross Mountain we shook our heads in disbelief and asked her if she realised just how difficult it would be. She nodded and remained determined.

She came with us by taxi to the foot of the mountain and I decided I would help her take a few steps upwards, although she had not sought any assistance. I took her left arm and we started out. I tried to pick the best spot for each of her steps expecting her to be happy to at least climb a short distance.

We kept going slowly, step by step and she showed no sign of stopping. I thought that if we could reach the first station of the cross that would be a miracle. We did and we prayed and we rested and she intimated that we should continue. That we did, and in due course we reached the second, then the third station and by then I was the one in need of rest.

Step by step, we wound our way without once looking up until suddenly we found ourselves at the top of the mountain and just in time for a special Mass which was being offered there. I thought the Lord was certainly making his presence felt. But then I began to think of how on earth we were going to manage going down as often one finds that the descent is even more dangerous than the ascent.

Well, the Lord walked down with us and everybody rejoiced. We got a taxi back to our place of residence in time for the evening meal. I am pleased to say that today, seven years later, Our Lady of the Climb is still going strong and well able to attend daily Mass in our local church.

In 2009, I joined a group from Connemara led by an tAthair Colm Ó Ceannabháin on a pilgrimage to Medjugorje. We had a very enriching time there. It was a relatively small group and we got to know one another well.

We prayed the Stations of the Cross, which were located close to the statue of the risen Christ and as we walked and prayed I became filled with emotion and sorrow for all the pain and suffering Our Lord had to go through to bring about our salvation. As we moved from station to station we sang a beautiful Gaelic song *Caoineadh na dTrí Múire* (*Lament of the Three Marys*), on the sorrows of Our Lady during the passion of Christ. Her son's face was so disfigured that at first sight she did not recognise him:

An é sin an maicín a d'iompair mé trí ráithe?
Óchón is óchón ó!

The more we sang and prayed, the more I cried and the better I felt. Throughout the week I was able to capture that expression of sorrow and enter into a mood of reflection and repentance. I returned home refreshed.

In May 2009 I felt the need to travel back again but I had no luck in finding a group that was going on a date that suited me. I was visiting Howth then and called into the church to see if I could get Mass. I was late for that and contented myself with a few prayers. On my way out I spotted a notice on the board about a trip to Medjugorje so I jotted down the contact number and, when I got a chance, I rang it.

A lady answered and when I enquired she was very apologetic and told me that all the seats had been booked up as it was so close to the departure date. She must have sensed my disappointment and finished off by saying, 'Leave me your name and number in case there is any last minute cancellation.' The lady was Maureen Maher from Sutton and she sounded a bit sad at not being able to accommodate me.

Five minutes later my phone rang and she was back to say that someone must have been praying for me. She had just found a seat. I would have to take it straight away. I had no hesitation in saying, 'Yes.' Our Lady was inviting me there.

I had a really special time on that trip and felt that the Holy Spirit was with us not just in prayer but also in the many chats we had about life and its many twists and turns.

I went to the Tuesday evening concert presented by David Parkes and found myself sitting beside Maureen, the leader of the group. On stage David was joined by Fr Liam Lawton who then dedicated a song to two little angels, one who had just entered heaven and one who had just arrived on earth.

Maureen had lost a daughter and my daughter had just given birth to a daughter. Both were Down's syndrome children. Maureen gave me a lot of useful information on the subject and also explained how such children can live full lives and give great joy to everybody around them. At that point I became aware of one of the reasons Our Lady had invited me to go with this particular group. As a mother, she was teaching me how to deal with life. There was another reason for bringing me there and that would emerge in the months ahead.

I had noticed on the trip that I wasn't quite as energetic as I had been. When I returned I threw myself back into music production, as I had been doing before, but my energy levels were down. We went to France in August to meet up with our friends Máire and Mícheál Ó hEidhin but I sensed at the time that something was wrong with my system.

When we returned from our holiday I went to my GP and he sent me to a specialist who told me I had a tumour and it was serious. I had a colonoscopy soon afterward and I was told to cancel the next four months. My mind was racing and I couldn't get my head around not been able to fulfill the many obligations I had made for those months.

Three days later it was confirmed that the tumour was malignant and I was diagnosed with bowel cancer. Up until then I had been hoping that the tumour was benign and now that hope was shattered. I tried to accept reality but I was still thinking that maybe it was all just a bad dream.

With the exception of the usual ailments I had enjoyed good health down through the years. True, I had been under a lot of pressure at work from time to time but I never once thought that I might wind up with this disease.

I struggled with myself and with the Lord for about three days and eventually I got the grace of acceptance, knelt down before the Sacred Heart and told God I would offer it all up and go with his will.

I was then ready to do battle.

Síle came with me each day to the hospital for the radiotherapy and the chemotherapy treatment. She found the daily routine just as hard as I did. She felt helpless and filled with worry but she bravely carried on, making sure she was waiting for me when I came out, irrespective of the time it took.

When it became known that I had been diagnosed with cancer many people began to petition the Lord on my behalf. Some came together in small groups and prayed for the duration of my illness. In fact, it would be true to say that they stormed heaven with their efforts. I will be forever grateful for the support I got from the community. It made me realise just how important people are in times of need.

By January of 2010, I was ready for theatre. It was tough on the surgeons as the affected section was hard to reach. However, the good news was that they had successfully removed a section and were confident they had got all of the cancer cells out. Over the following months I made a slow but steady recovery.

During this time we got an invitation to join a group led by Fr John Hogan going in May to Turin where the Holy Shroud was on view to the public for a short time. Fr John had founded an association dedicated to St Genesius, patron saint of those working in the theatrical and cinematic sectors and we were members. We opted to go with the group even though I was due to have an operation the following month to reverse the stoma I had from my previous operation.

In Turin we joined the waiting crowds outside the Cathedral and were led into an area were a short film was shown, giving the history of the shroud and indicating were the marks of the body and the face could be seen. We then moved into the church where the shroud of some 14 ft in length was draped across and above the altar. Knowing how to interpret it, we focused on one area and suddenly we were looking at the face of Jesus Christ. It was a very gripping experience and one that we can recall again and again. We had a good twenty minutes to spend in the church, which allowed us to view the shroud from different angles. The visit gave us a wonderful opportunity to dwell on our Lord's passion and death and to further strengthen our faith.

Recent work on the shroud had given artists a chance to paint the face of Jesus in a new way and one which properly represented his countenance. These were done in colour and in different sizes so we each bought a selection to bring home. We felt privileged to have been there and grateful to Fr John for all his work in arranging the trip.

My operation in June was supposed to involve between five and seven days in hospital. Little did I realise at the time what was to come. Within a week it became clear that my system was not working according to plan and so another operation was carried out.

My body couldn't take it and I duly collapsed. My family were called in while the medical team worked on me and brought me back from the brink. However, other complications set in and I struggled for weeks, getting weaker by the day. While I was reluctant to admit defeat I got to the point where I just wanted to lie there under the blanket, undisturbed.

However, God had a different plan and a new doctor appeared at my bedside, began working on me physically and psychologically and so hope returned. In a matter of a few weeks I had turned the corner and was temporally discharged, having spent over ten weeks of the summer period in a hospital bed.

I was in and out of hospital several times between then and the following January (2011). At that stage the doctors decided to operate again and, if necessary, remove my large intestine. The operation continued for most of the day, at which time the surgeons felt that they had done everything they could to correct the many problems they had encountered. The ordeal left me very weak but with the hope that I would have a chance to rebuild my battered body once again.

I was discharged a few weeks later. I was very frail, just skin and bones and all I wanted to do was stay in bed. After ten days of this I realised that I was going nowhere. Prompted by my guardian angel I gave myself a stern warning that action was required. I just had to find a way to motivate myself.

I tried to do some simple things like listening to music, reading, watching TV, but I had no interest in anything. I was just down in body, mind and spirit.

I decided to set myself some simple task that I could measure and hopefully build on, like steps. I walked down the corridor, five steps down and five back, then rested. Five minutes later I repeated the exercise. That was enough for the first day. After a couple of days I was slowly walking around the house. Then a few days later I took a couple of steps outside. In another week or so I was taking a few steps along the lane and was now at the start of the long road to recovery.

In October of 2011, I was back in Medjugorje with Maureen's group. I was hoping that I would be strong enough to climb part or all of Apparition Hill. Sure enough on the second attempt I went all the way. The company I was with was very encouraging and I grew stronger in body and in spirit with every passing day. So now my thoughts turned to Cross Mountain, the big one.

I knew that the climb, with the Stations of the Cross en route, was in the schedule. I thought that perhaps if I could reach the first station and then turn around, I would feel that I had accomplished something useful.

When the day came and we started to climb I found the going very tough. I wondered if I should stop and rest halfway to the first station. I slowed down but kept moving and managed to reach it trailing at the end of the group. I sat on a rock and listened to the prayers and the beat of my pounding heart.

I had to decide whether to continue for a little bit longer or turn back. The respite gave me time to get my breath back and I felt some of my strength returning. I also thought of the day, seven years previously, when I helped the elderly lady to conquer the same mountain. I decided to try going on as the next station was a much shorter distance than the first.

Joe Casey was one of my companions on the climb. He had some concerns about the way ahead also, but when I saw that he was making an effort and succeeding I decided that I should follow suit. We walked together for a while and I found myself at the next station. My strength grew with each step and before I realised it we were at the top as though we had been carried there. My confidence got a big boost that day.

One thing I learned on the journey was that you need God at all times. I remember praying for help while on the climb. Help would come but then I would temporarily forget about God and think I could do this on my own. As soon as the thought hit me I would stumble and nearly fall so I soon realised that the Lord was teaching me a very valuable lesson.

Looking back over recent events, I realise that God had a plan for me. It was not the plan that I had in my mind but one that would achieve his wishes to keep us close to him. I am aware now that in fulfilling his plan one receives many graces and blessings.

Just before I fell ill our daughter gave birth to her second child, a girl. We were told that there were complications and that the doctors would be keeping her in hospital for some time. They said that she was a Down's syndrome baby, which was a surprise to all of us and something we knew nothing about.

However, within a couple of weeks she was allowed home prior to operations on her heart and subject to careful monitoring. Her extended family bonded together, spreading love and affection and giving one another courage and hope. Katie grew in strength, the operations were postponed and then cancelled as the holes in her heart closed and other complications seemed to fade away.

Soon after she was born I was inspired to write a piece of music in her honour, which my daughter Éilís and I, together with Steve Cooney, recorded. Soon after that we had the opportunity to include it in an album to raise funds for Our Lady's Hospital for Sick Children in Dublin. The piece is called *Katie, Katie, Cara mo Chroí* and is in the format of a planxty.

Katie is progressing well and recently celebrated her 3rd birthday. She is a great source of happiness to all of us and brings the best out of people. We are learning a lot from her, just as God had planned.

When I was at my lowest in the summer of 2010, I kept a picture of the face of Our Lord by my bedside, one I had brought back from Turin. During the long sleepless nights in hospital that summer I felt the presence of the Lord beside my bed, watching over me and giving me comfort and solace. I was buoyed up by the images I brought home from our visit to the shroud a few months earlier.

The day before my major operation in January 2011 I thought it would be good to make my confession but I didn't know where I would find a priest as the chaplain of the hospital was not available. I did see a priest in another part of the ward but he was fully occupied attending to other people.

However Síle, who was attending evening Mass in Spiddal, asked our parish priest, An tAthair Seán Mac Aodha, to remember me in his prayers at Mass the following morning. He said yes of course but that he would like to drop in on me that night and so he did. He heard my confession, and gave me the last rites.

Soon after he left I felt that a deep peace had descended upon me and was within me and around me. I had been told that I needed sleep to prepare me for the next day but I was not hopeful as I had only fitful sleep for weeks on end and the doctors would not prescribe sleeping tablets prior to the operation.

I fell into a trance and a deep sleep and when I was awoken at around six o'clock in preparation for my visit to the theatre I still had this strong feeling of complete happiness and lack of worry.

The operation lasted most of the day. I awoke briefly that evening to nod to Síle and my family and went back to sleep. In the middle of the night, while still in Intensive Care, I sensed that something strange was happening to me. I glanced through half-open eyelids and saw to my left the outline of someone holding my arm high in the air. I wondered what on earth was happening.

Wide awake I looked up and saw a man in a white coat holding my fingers against his and looking intently at them. 'What could the problem be?' I wondered to myself. 'Your fingers are much longer than mine,' he said with curiosity.

I pondered at the relevance of this to my condition as I was more concerned with the outcome of the operation.

He then said, 'Do you by any chance play the piano?' I nodded weakly in agreement and this seemed to surprise him greatly. 'Oh what a coincidence,' he said with great enthusiasm. I had to smile.

He was a male nurse who had been watching over me through the night. He was from Germany and had a great interest in music. We talked for some time about music and this made me forget about myself. I still smile when I think of the incident. God has a great sense of humour.

11

Honor Taylor

Honor Taylor was on a summer vacation in Croatia when she went for a day trip to the village of Medjugorje. Instantly impressed by the place, Honor couldn't wait to get back and has been to Medjugorje over twenty-two times since. When deep in prayer on Križevac one day, Honor heard a voice that gave a simple but meaningful message to her.

This is Honor's testimony.

I first heard about Medjugorje from a lady who used to help me in my home. It would have been back in the early days and although I was interested in what the lady was telling me about the place, I really didn't pay it too much heed.

However, in 1989, I went on holidays to a resort near Medjugorje and I remember that while I was there I kept thinking that I would love to go visit the village.

So, the following year in 1990, I headed off again to the same resort for a holiday. I happened to have my four children with me on the trip and things had been very difficult in my life around this time.

This difficulty stemmed from my early life and I had lots of unhappy times. I was in a particularly dark place and I had done things in my life that I shouldn't have done. I had returned to my church and felt forgiven but I still had lots of troubles and was having a very difficult time.

During my holiday, myself and the children took a day trip up to Medjugorje and I just found it to be the most extraordinary place. We went to the 10 o'clock Mass and the atmosphere in the church was one of immense peace and holiness.

When we went into the church, it was so packed with people. I remember thinking that you would never see this in Ireland. The Franciscan priests took my two youngest children by the hand and brought them up to the altar and the choir was singing *How Great Thou Art*.

I immediately felt peace overwhelming me, as well as joy and calmness. It was amazing to see all the many priests concelebrating Mass on the altar. The reverence in the church was powerful and there was a real feeling that God was close.

I went up and received the Eucharist and when I did I felt nothing but total joy. I went back to my seat and remember tears flowing down my face. I wasn't at all embarrassed about it and I was oblivious to everybody else.

We were scheduled to go back to the hotel but the organisers of the day trip asked if anybody wanted to stay on for the apparition. Most people, including me, voted to stay on.

The place was crowded and we all stepped aside when the visionaries came. People started to pray the rosary in all the different languages – French, German, and Italian.

We all joined in, even though I wasn't very familiar with the rosary. Although I came from a Catholic upbringing, we didn't practice religion much in the home.

As we were praying the rosary, the sun seemed to spin in the sky. The colours of the rainbow permeated from the sun and people were deep in prayer. My son was only seventeen at the time and when I looked at him, he too was praying the rosary. It was both beautiful and extraordinary.

When it was over, we all got back on the coach and finished off our holiday on the coast. All I kept thinking of was how I was going to get back there. I came home and, although things were still very difficult for me, I felt that I had received huge grace out in Medjugorje.

I longed for daily Mass and for the Eucharist; something that I had never felt before.

I went back that autumn with a group from my parish and we arrived to the most horrendous thunder storm, forked lightning, strong winds and torrential rain. When we were driving into the village in our little bus I was thinking to myself: 'Oh no, this is not what I wanted at all.'

I was beginning to think that I had made a mistake by coming and that I really didn't want to be here at all. Everyone was praying on the bus and I really didn't think I was going to be able to handle it all.

However, there was a friend in the group with me and she really helped me during the coming days. I just wasn't in the spirit at all but I had made the commitment to come and I decided that I would see it through.

I went along to all the services and met Fr Slavko. I was very moved by the Adoration and the Masses yet I still felt it was all too much. Some people were fasting and I thought that maybe I was after taking on too much. I doubted my own spiritual dimension in the whole thing and felt that maybe I just wasn't holy enough. I felt like I was just peeping into the door of Our Lord and wasn't able to go in.

By Wednesday, the sun came and the place dried up and I began to pray more and felt more rested.

We went up Križevac, the big mountain, and although I didn't want to go initially as I felt I wasn't fit enough, my friend urged me to climb it with her.

We both fell back from the group and we prayed Fr Slavko's book of the Way of the Cross. Halfway up the mountain, at one of the stations, we were kneeling down and my friend began to pray especially for me and my own family. It was very emotional as she named each of my children through her prayers. I also started to pray and then the most extraordinary thing happened.

I was praying from my heart and then there was a silence. I thought that one of the group had come back down to us and was speaking to us as I heard a man's voice. It was the most beautiful gentle voice and it said, 'Be not afraid, I go before you always.'

I turned around and there was no one there. It wasn't an interior voice and it was not imagined. It was as if I had a headset on and was listening to a CD – it was an audible voice.

I said it to my friend and she didn't show too much amazement when I told her because I think she may have had her own experience too. I knew that it was Jesus speaking to me.

Suddenly, I had a new energy and climbed up to the top of the mountain and really wanted to stay there at the cross. I put my head down and prayed from the heart and I think that was the first time that I had really opened up because I received this wonderful grace.

We came down the mountain and I felt so euphorically happy.

Years later, I met a lady who had seen me on the mountain that day. She asked me what had happened to me so I told her my story. She said that she knew something special had happened to me because I looked so happy that I seemed as though I was on fire with the Holy Spirit.

I really didn't want to leave Medjugorje but, of course, I knew I had to go back home. I came back to just the same, if not more problems at home.

Over the years, it was through Medjugorje that I learned to cope with my personal problems. I have been back over twenty-two times.

I'm not saying that everything is wonderful now with my life but only for Medjugorje I don't know where I would be. People need to go to the village to experience it for themselves. You can find fault with everything and people complain about the commercialism but it is the most extraordinary and holy place.

Every time I come home I say that I won't go again that year but I always give in and end up making another trip.

I love Croatia and Bosnia and Herzegovina but when I get to Medjugorje I feel like I am home and I think the Holy Mother is just waiting for people to go there.

When you are there you need to open your heart and be prepared, maybe even for difficulties, but then the grace comes and your whole life can be turned around.

What does Medjugorje mean to me?

It is a small taste of heaven on earth with beautiful Masses, spiritual music, wonderful nature and people. When the priests come through the crowds with the monstrance you can see people reaching out. It is like Jesus himself is walking through the crowds as he did when he lived on earth.

We all struggle through life but in Medjugorje there is an anointing to be had. You can get away from the group or the crowds and go and have some time for yourself and ask the Blessed Mother to bring you to Jesus. You can go to confession and you shouldn't feel afraid – no matter what you have done in your life. It is like an encounter with Jesus in forgiveness. We all have people who we need to forgive and we all need to be forgiven and, in this way, we can be healed of painful memories.

You have to live in the moment because that is all you have.

Medjugorje is like intensive care for the soul. You can let go of all your worries and it brings a peace that you can't receive anywhere else.

I was filled with self doubt and felt that through my life I had been very far away from God. I had strayed off the path, particularly in my youth; but nobody is beyond redemption and each person is precious in God's eyes. He is just waiting for you to come back.

12

Ollie Clarke

Ollie Clarke is a radio DJ with Spirit FM. When he got the opportunity to visit Medjugorje for the first time, he found himself speaking of his experience on live radio in the village.

This is Ollie's testimony.

It was in 1995 that I went to Medjugorje for the first time. I did not know anything at all about Medjugorje. It was a lady friend who told to me about this beautiful place and how Our Lady was appearing there each day.

This sounded really great to me as I had just been converted through Our Lady a couple of months before. It was an American woman called Maria Serocco with messages from Our Lady of Garabandal that helped me in my conversion, but that is another story.

My lady friend informed me that she was going to Medjugorje and she asked me whether or not I was going. I told her that at that time I wouldn't have the money to go, as she was going that week. To my surprise this lady said, 'That's OK. I'll pay for your trip.'

I was so humbled by her offer as she was giving me this chance to go to Medjugorje. We were on the plane on the way to Medjugorje when a thought struck me: 'What am I doing here? I'm going to be praying all week and climbing mountains. What am I doing here?'

Anyway, we arrived in Medjugorje and as the week progressed I found that my heart was being opened more to the love of Our Holy Mother and to Jesus. I climbed the mountains with the pilgrimage group and also alone.

I was amazed by the humbleness of the people of Medjugorje and how peaceful and content they were. The people had very little and were happy, whereas I had enough but still was not at peace.

On one of the days, a radio station from Mostar visited Medjugorje and the leader of our group was asked to speak on it and she wanted someone else from the group to speak with her, so they elected me to speak with her.

I remember the interviewer asking me questions as to why I came to Medjugorje. My answer was that Our Holy Mother had brought me here as a gift to show me that she loves me. He asked me was I not afraid as there was war in their country. I said plainly, 'No, as Our Holy Mother brought peace to our country and she will bring peace to yours.'

Later that week I was in Mostar bringing clothes and blankets to the poor people affected by war. These people wanted to meet this guy who they heard on the radio, who spoke peacefully about their Gospa (Our Lady).

I went home with peace in my heart; full of a hope and joy that words cannot explain. On my second visit to Medjugorje I felt that I was now returning the gift to Our Lady by paying my own way. I gave thanks to her for having shown me her love and peace, and that of her son Jesus.

On this visit, Our Lady told me to share the peace and love with all those whom I meet. She also urged that when I return to Ireland that I keep the message of Medjugorje alive in my heart. I understood what she meant. I returned every year after, bringing groups of people with me to Medjugorje and to date I have been there twenty-seven times.

Each year, Our Lady never ceases to show her love for me. I have fallen in love with the beautiful people and it's like I'm returning home to see my relations. The experiences I have had in Medjugorje have given me the most wonderful sense of the presence of Our Holy Mother and her caring way for all her children; that God is real and he wants to help us return to his kingdom.

The great Adoration ceremony that takes place in Medjugorje really lifts me up and fills me with great joy and peace. I have learned that in the great silence of your heart is where you hear God's voice speak to you. I have met people from all over the world and am constantly amazed at how we can live as one.

What does Medjugorje mean to me?

If I was to relate Medjugorje to a Bible event I would say that it is close to the wedding feast of Cana. When the guests ran out of the wine they turned to Our Blessed Mother, who interceded on their behalf to Jesus. She returned with the message: 'Do whatever he tells you.'

That is what is happening there today. Our Lady is saying to us through her messages and the visionaries, 'Do whatever he tells you.' So each time I visit Medjugorje I am given a greater insight into the wisdom of God and how to live his gospel message.

13

Fr Ruairí Ó Domhnaill

Fr Ruairí Ó Domhnaill was only sixteen years of age when he visited Medju-gorje for the first time. Two years later, at the age of eighteen, he made the decision to enter the priesthood. Events that happened in Medjugorje during that first visit were the catalyst in making him decide to dedicate his life to this vocation.

This is Fr Ruairí's testimony.

I was about fourteen years of age when I first heard of Medjugorje. Neighbours of ours went and their son was one of my best friends. They were a big family but were not overly religious or regular Mass-goers. Someone had convinced the parents to go to Medjugorje and when they came back, their son kept saying to me, 'God, you won't believe the difference in my parents since they came home from their pilgrimage.' He said they were fasting twice a week and going to Mass every day. This made me a little bit curious.

But I also remember my mother coming home one day with two typed sheets of paper that someone had given her detailing what was happening in Medjugorje. It said that Our Lady was saying that we needed to say fifteen decades of the rosary a day. We were already, as a family, praying five decades of the rosary every day, and that was enough of a struggle for us. I took the two pieces of paper and when my mother wasn't looking, I put them up onto the top of the press, hoping she would forget about them. I knew that if she got it into her head, then we would indeed be praying those fifteen decades of the rosary!

I grew up in a very religious household but it was also a household that was very republican. For me, religion was just part of my Irish identity. The speaking of Irish was very much encouraged and I excelled in this subject at school. We sang all the Republican songs. If we started a song and didn't know the words, my father would send us off to learn the song. The practice of our faith was part of that identity. I wasn't involved in the parish in any way and I was never an altar server but we prayed the rosary every day and both my parents were daily Mass-goers.

At school, I was always having rows with my religion teacher and it would be over things such as the IRA and republicanism. I think the priest who taught me religion was quite shocked at the books I was reading and my whole outlook on such issues.

One day in religion class, totally out of the blue, he turned to me and asked, 'Have you ever heard of Medjugorje?'

This was in the middle of a row and I turned to him and said, 'Well, yes, these neighbours of mine have been there.'

He said, 'Well, if you go to Medjugorje, it will change all your beliefs and your way of thinking.'

A few days later, I was in the school yard and the same priest approached me and asked me to tell him again how I had heard of Medjugorje. He then asked me if I had any interest in going myself. I told him that I would be interested in going and when he said he was going that Easter, I decided to save up for the trip and go along with him.

As the departure date approached it turned out that the priest couldn't travel as his mother was unwell. It was 1986 and at sixteen years of age I found myself booked in to go to Medjugorje with a group of strangers. At this time, Medjugorje was behind the Iron Curtain and a communist country and my parents were up the walls with worry. I truly believed in what was happening out there, even at that stage, so I was determined to go on the trip.

I went out at Easter in 1986, stayed for one week and it just blew me away. It was the complete changing point in my life. It turned everything upside down for me – everything I believed, everything I thought and everything I wanted to do.

When I came home, I remember going to Mass with my brother that Saturday evening. He turned to me and said, 'Ruairí, stop doing that!'

I turned to him and said, 'Stop what?'

He replied, 'Stop smiling at everyone!'

I came home so happy from Medjugorje and it really had a profound effect on me. My mother also told me that my older brother and sister had sat her down one day and asked her what had happened to me; that I was a completely different person.

Everyone was asking me what I saw – did I see this or did I see that. People spoke about the peace over in Medjugorje but to me 'peace' was a passive word. What I experienced was more active and deeper. It was a bit frustrating when I came home because I couldn't articulate to people what I felt.

A few weeks later I was at Mass and the reading was The Road to Emmaus in which the two disciples are leaving Jerusalem and they encounter Jesus along the way. When the priest read out the line where one of the disciples says to the other, 'Did our hearts not burn within us on that road?' it was like a bolt out of the blue. That was exactly what Medjugorje felt like for me – my heart began to burn with desire.

When my parents collected me from the airport, they were asking me, 'What was it, what was it?' I replied to them by saying that God and Mary were so real to me in Medjugorje, you almost felt that if you reached out, you would touch them. There was a strong sense of the presence of God out there.

Previously, I had no sense of a relationship between God and me, even though prayers were said. I always thought that charismatic people were quite stupid; I mean, why do you need to put your hands in the air when you were praying to God? But when in Medjugorje I began to understand that when something touches your heart this is something you do.

Before I travelled to Medjugorje, I had begun to wonder about the priesthood but I never really believed that God could be calling me to the vocation. Priests were put on such a pedestal that I just didn't think it was for me.

Towards the end of my week in Medjugorje, I was sitting in a café when a woman came in and asked us if we had heard what had happened the previous night. Apparently the links on some other woman's rosary beads had turned gold. Of course, we all put our hands in our pockets and took out our beads but everyone's were still silver.

From the café, we ventured up to the presbytery where Our Lady was appearing at that time. We were all kneeling outside during the apparition and when it was over, a lady in our group came over to me. She was crying and told me that during the apparition, she had glanced over at me. She said that all of a sudden, it was like I was in a tunnel of light and that she heard a woman's voice, in her ear that said, 'He is going to be a priest.'

I was so shocked by this and I went straight over to confession with Fr Svet. I told my confession and afterward he asked me what I was going to do with my life. So, I told him what had just happened with the woman and he turned to me and said that I should go for it because 'we need you'. I was given a decade of the rosary for my penance and I went over to the side of the church to kneel down and pray. When I took the same pair of rosary beads out of my pocket, which I had looked at only half an hour earlier, I noticed that the links on the chain had changed to gold.

Prior to that, if I had plucked up the courage to go for the priesthood I would never have lasted through the seminary because I just didn't have that confidence. But I felt God had given me these two signs – the lady and the gold beads.

I went back to Medjugorje the following October after saving every penny I could. I brought two friends with me and we were walking through the fields one particular day when we met three women kneeling in the fields looking up at the sun. They asked us if we could see the sun spinning and I replied by saying that if you looked at the sun for long enough it more than likely would spin.

One of the women got particularly annoyed and angry with me and she said, 'What's the point in coming to Medjugorje if you don't have any faith?' I said nothing and walked off but the next day I met two of the other women and they asked me if I had seen their friend; that she wanted to talk to me. I thought that maybe she wanted to apologise but I hadn't seen her until then.

Later on that week, I met her and she said to me, 'I need to tell you what happened to me on that day. I was so angry with you and as you walked away I said in my mind, "God why do people like that come here who don't have any faith?"' She told me that after she said this, she heard a voice that said, 'Yes, but he is going to be a priest.'

I had confirmation of my intended vocation twice in the one year – both times in Medjugorje.

I went back to Medjugorje every year and knew in my heart that I was going to enter the priesthood. At eighteen years of age, I wasn't sure who to talk to about it so I told a priest in my school. He set up the meetings for me but one piece of advice he gave me was not to mention Medjugorje. He knew me well and knew how significant Medjugorje had been and I remember saying to him, 'How on earth can I do this? How can I talk about my faith journey and not about Medjugorje?'

He said, 'Ruairi, believe me – whatever you do, do not mention Medjugorje.'

So, I went for the interviews and met the vocations director twice. At the second meeting he told me that I was still a bit young and maybe I should go to college for a year or travel and see the world. I was also trying to explain to him my calling to the priesthood without mentioning Medjugorje.

I had put down three referees on my application form and the vocations director commented on one of the names by asking me if I had thought the third priest on the list was a bit strange. I asked him what he meant by this and he replied by saying, 'Oh he is always flying off to that place in Yugoslavia.' He asked me how I knew him and I told him that I actually met him in Medjugorje. He sat back and asked me what I thought of it and so I told him how I felt.

The following week he went to meet my parents. I came home that night and my parents were sitting at the fire. I had previously told them that the vocations director had wanted me to take the year out but when I came in they told me that he had wanted me to begin studying for the priesthood that September. I was shocked because I was sure he was quite adamant that I take a year before making any decision.

A few months later, I met another priest who knew the vocations director and he had told him that he was indeed going to get me to spend a year in college but the way I articulated myself around the whole subject of Medjugorje made him decide that I was ready. It was definitely Medjugorje that got me through the door.

Since then, I have gone every year. I usually go once with a group from my parish and once on my own. Going as a priest is a completely different experience. It is such a profound experience to hear confession over there.

When people come in and kneel down and tell me their story, I often feel that I am the one that should be kneeling. The confessions boxes out there can be quite hot but I have regularly sat there for four, five or six hours at a time and I always come out on a high. It is such a profound and spiritual experience hearing confession out there. It is really quite extraordinary.

All through my priesthood, I have lived through the scandals of the Catholic Church in Ireland. Bishop Casey resigned when I was in my second year in the seminary and after that it went from bad to worse. Going to Medjugorje for all those years has renewed me and my faith and it gives me that boost I need.

When I go now, people ask me if I still feel the same peace but I really love bringing people out who have never been there before and seeing the transformation in them out there. I am a vocations director now myself and I meet a lot of young Irish men who are considering the priesthood and Medjugorje is a huge factor in these young men making their final decision.

I can remember a priest friend of mine who was made vocations director in his parish and the bishop had told him that he didn't want any 'Medjugorje vocations'. He told me after, that if it wasn't for these 'Medjugorje vocations' there wouldn't be any new priests.

I have been present a few times at Ivan's apparitions and it is not as though I feel anything in particular but I am happy just to be there and know that Our Lady is present.

I knew another priest who had said to me before that he thought Eucharistic Adoration was 'medieval superstition'. He also had no belief and no interest in Medjugorje.

When I walked into a bookshop one day, he was there with another priest who goes to Medjugorje regularly. I asked the other priest when he was going out next and then turned jokingly to the sceptic priest and asked him when he was going out. When I commented that I was going out in June, he told me that he might come with me. I was really surprised but held him to it and rang him a few weeks later. He began to backtrack but I hounded him until he eventually agreed to come out with me.

When he came out, he really took a backseat and didn't dress as a priest or concelebrate at any of the Masses. We were invited to Ivan's for the apparition and we were all jammed into this small room. The priest was very quiet afterward and on the way back to the house I was almost afraid to ask him how he felt. I went off to the church and he told me he wanted to go off for a walk. Later that night we met up and were chatting about different things. I asked him what he thought of Ivan's apparition that day. He told me that without even being told, he knew exactly when Our Lady had appeared and he knew exactly when she was gone.

What does Medjugorje mean to me?

For me there is life before Medjugorje and there is life after Medjugorje. That first week, when I was only sixteen years of age, had such a profound impact on me; it changed me completely. It changed the way I thought and all my priorities and it set a direction for me in this life – a life and vocation in the priesthood.

14

Des Kelly

*Des Kelly is known for his successful flooring and furniture retail shops.
During the boom years, Des admits that he became consumed by materialistic
things and began to drink heavily. When his wife asked him to go on a pilgrimage to Medjugorje he was very reluctant as it was at the same time as the World
Cup. Over there, Des discovered the power of prayer and was healed from his
addiction to alcohol. He now dedicates a lot of his time to helping others with
addiction.*

This is Des' testimony.

I was born and reared in Dublin's inner city and I had eleven brothers
and sisters. We lost a boy and a girl in the early days which left nine of
us and my parents. My father worked hard as a coalman in the city
and he was a good man – a pioneer and non-smoker all his life. He was
uneducated and a humble man but he worked extremely hard to try
and provide for us all.

Our parish was St Francis Xavier's Church in Gardiner Street which
was run by the Jesuits. It was a terrific church and I went to school close
by in Gardiner Street School. From there, I went to St Canice's school on
the North Circular Road and never missed a day nor was I ever late.
However, I left at twelve and a half and I could barely read or write.

It wasn't the Christian Brothers' fault or anything; in fact great schol-
ars had come out of that school and indeed out of my class. Personally,
I just wasn't really into learning. I just wanted to work with my father
at the coal and he was also a pig farmer and I wanted to help out with
that too.

We were very privileged in that we had the Gardiner Street church
beside us and there were terrific missions in there. It was a very spiritual
area and there was something about the Catholic Church there that was
really fantastic. There was a lot happening in the church back then. The
Christian Brothers were very good at teaching religion too in school.

All I wanted to do was work, so at lunchtime I would come home
and get my box car and push it around the back lanes and collect all the
waste to give to the pigs, and then I would rush back to school.

I did the exam to go to tech school and I remember going over to St Francis Xavier's Church beforehand and I asked God to guide me and protect me for this exam. But I had no chance and, of course, I failed.

I left school then and got a job as an electrician for twelve months but I had no future there because I didn't get my apprenticeship.

My mother's family were all working in Aer Rianta, in the airport, and so I decided to go for a position there. Again, I had to do a simple exam and so I went back over to the same church again, got Mass and Holy Communion and I prayed that God would help me get the job. I didn't get it, however, and I began wondering whether God was listening to me at all. At the same time, I still had great respect for Him and Our Lady.

I moved on in life and worked for my father and then in a haulage business for a few years. I met my wife, Youlanda, and we moved into a little flat on Cork Street and we began buying and selling furniture. We opened our first shop in Sallins, Co. Kildare and had nine children, one of whom we sadly lost.

I was very successful in the carpet business and I got carried away with greed and more materialistic things began to take over in my life. I began buying property and as I went along and got more successful, I opened more shops. I always still loved God and Our Lady and St Joseph but I drifted away and had more time for material things than for God.

I always made sure we went to Mass every week as a family with the kids but I wasn't really happy as I went along in life.

My wife, Youlanda, would visit the various shrines every year including Lourdes and Fatima, as well as Medjugorje. I never went with her as I was always tied up with work.

In 1998, my wife was due to head off on a pilgrimage to Medjugorje with a friend of hers but then the woman's brother died very suddenly. The World Cup was on that year and my wife asked me would I go with her to Medjugorje. I told her that I wasn't sure and she said that I needed a change and that I was coming and that was it!

Reluctantly, I went to Medjugorje and my wife was telling me not to worry about seeing the World Cup and that there were plenty of televisions that I could watch the matches on. I would go to daily Mass and then go and find a place to watch the matches and I really didn't do much more. My wife was a bit disappointed with me because I was drinking so much. A priest who was in our group, Fr Aidan Carroll, was having a few prayer meetings in the house we were staying in and he was also doing a bit of healing, which I really enjoyed.

I couldn't believe there were so many people out in Medjugorje and that they were so happy. My wife seemed to know everybody out there and they would stop her in the street and she would introduce me. I felt so relaxed and everybody was happy and I remember thinking, 'Oh my God, what is going on here?'

Later on in the week, I met another priest called Fr Peter Mary Rookey who was also doing some healing. My wife knew the priest because our eldest granddaughter is blind and my wife often brought her to this priest when he was over in Ireland. Fr Rookey did some healing on me while I was there.

I was starting to enjoy myself and I couldn't believe how happy people were, going around with rosary beads in their hands and socialising in Colombo's and saying the rosary. I felt that there really must be something here.

When I came home from Medjugorje, I started asking God to guide me and to teach me how to pray and have peace. I asked him to help me get these materialistic things and alcohol out of my life so I could be happy like my wife and the other people in Medjugorje. I asked him to put his mantle around me and guide me and show me the way.

When I came home from this first trip, I felt guilty about and ashamed of my drinking, and of sometimes making a fool of myself because of it. I was also ashamed of the effect the hangovers were having on my performance in my daily life.

I started praying to the Venerable Matt Talbot (who was a chronic alcoholic) for help. I felt an affinity with him as I had grown up in number 24 Rutland Street and he had lived in number 18 Upper Rutland Street. I always remember as a boy of about nine or ten years of age that the Legion of Mary would pray and say the rosary in Matt Talbot's old room every Sunday, as part of their effort to have him canonised.

I would go up to these prayer meetings and I remember that our street felt very alive in those days and that there was a lot of interest in Matt Talbot and in the effort to get him canonised. Visitors would come from all over the world and there was a sense of great pride in our community and its association with Matt Talbot, which I myself felt also.

As a result of this affinity with Matt Talbot I started to pray to him for guidance and strength, to help me in my effort to give up drink.

My prayers were answered and in September 2001 I took the pledge for the rest of my life. I remember the last drink I had was watching Galway beat Meath in the All-Ireland final that year.

I am a much happier and contented person for having made that choice and I am forever grateful to Matt Talbot, Our Lady and God for answering my prayers in that regard.

I am now on the committee that promotes the cause of the Venerable Matt Talbot's canonisation. It would be great to see the people of Ireland, and of Dublin in particular, getting behind the cause to have Matt Talbot canonised. I think people would be amazed at how praying for such good things, and indeed how the power of prayer in general, can help them in their own lives. I have, from experience, great faith in the power of prayer.

A while after coming home from Medjugorje the first time, my wife and I were going down to Wexford for a holiday and when we stopped for a bite to eat in New Ross, we met a priest who my wife knew, called Fr Adrian Crowley. He told us he was opening a Cenacolo centre for addiction in Knock and asked if we could donate some furniture. My wife said that we would and asked him what he needed. He said they could do with some bunk beds and so we sent some down to Knock a few days later.

Fr Adrian rang to thank me and asked if I would like to come to Knock and meet Sister Elvira who was the nun from Italy who founded Cenacolo originally.

I was still drinking, although I knew it was wrong, and I was not very happy. I was still looking for contentment and peace in my life. I took the weekend off and myself and my wife went down and we met with Sr Elvira and looked around the house. I was totally blown away when I met Sr Elvira. She was so saintly and reminded me of Mother Teresa.

I really feel God started to open doors for me down there because I met a man called Frank Walsh who told me that he had bought his first carpet from me some years back. He asked me was I doing anything the following Wednesday. I told him I wasn't and so he asked me would I come down to the Morning Star Hostel and help out. I asked him what would I be doing and he told me I would be helping the homeless. I was delighted with this and Frank and I just seemed to click so I made arrangements to meet and help out.

There were a lot of good people there, feeding the men and giving a help out in the kitchen. We said the rosary at 7 p.m. and then again at 9 p.m. I thought all this was fantastic and so I continued to go there and I really enjoyed it.

From there I joined the Legion of Mary and then got involved with Cenacolo. I think God really opened those doors for me. I feel that when I was younger I never really lost my faith but I just got carried away with the material things in life. But I feel that God certainly opened doors because I became much happier and contented and I became a better husband and father. I really feel my prayers were answered. I'm now a director of Cenacolo and give a lot of my time to the community and I am glad to do it.

I never realised that my prayers would actually be answered. I had prayed for my exams and for the job in the airport and although I didn't get them God gave me something else; he gave me the gift of common sense and taught me the art of buying and selling. I have met really great people and it is so good to be part of all that. I feel like I am trying to catch up on lost time now with God. I would do anything for God; I would take a bullet for him.

It took me six months to get my head around things when I came home from Medjugorje the first time but now I just can't seem to get enough of it. Medjugorje is a special place; it is so peaceful. You meet people there who are your friends for life. There is so much to do there and I go as often as I can.

I never witnessed any miracle but I experienced the presence of God, Our Lady and St Joseph. Before I went to Medjugorje, I used to go to Spain or Portugal but I never go there anymore. Every chance I get, I go to Medjugorje and in the past I have travelled out there four or five times a year.

I know there are challenging times ahead but I could not function without God or the Catholic Church. I can't understand how any business person can survive or function without God and Our Blessed Lady.

I go to Medjugorje to recharge my batteries and to me it is like heaven. The sacrament of Reconciliation out there is amazing and I remember a priest hearing my confession and then I met with him for a coffee and a chat afterward. I asked him how I could rid my life of materialism and concentrate just on God, who is more important at the end of the day. He told me that the materialistic attitude in Irish society stems from the days of the famine; we all want our own home and to protect our families and we should not blame ourselves too much because it is normal in Irish society for us to want more in case we run short.

However, I wanted to get materialism out of my head and concentrate solely on God, who I really can't do enough for at this time in my life.

My wife and I were to travel out to Medjugorje together for Holy Week in Easter 2012. The night before we were due to fly, my wife turned to me and told me that she couldn't find my passport anywhere. I told her not to worry and that we would get up early in the morning and have a look for it. The next morning, there was a bit of panic and I could see my wife getting a bit agitated. I have a little altar in my room and I prayed intensely to St Anthony and felt that whatever would be would be. I had resigned myself to thinking that Youlanda would fly out that day and that I would simply follow on later.

I went back downstairs and when my wife took out what she thought was her passport, she opened it and realised it was mine after all. I couldn't believe it; the tables had really turned full circle and I ended up being the one who flew out to Medjugorje that day and Yolanda followed me out four days later.

However, it was almost a blessing in disguise as I had the most wonderful four days on my own. I met three lads from Waterford and we all just clicked and I took them off to see the Cenacolo of Medjugorje. I climbed the mountains and prayed hard and really felt like I was in heaven. I will always remember those few days on my own and what I got out of it. I remember thinking that if heaven is half as good as this, then we will be fine. No one has ever come back to tell us what heaven is like, but I imagine it would be like Medjugorje. There was so much peace and tranquility there.

I used to think that God wasn't really hearing my prayers but they were most certainly answered throughout my life and I always encourage people to pray and ask for help. Their prayers will be answered, no matter what happens.

A close friend of mine died a short time ago and I had him in Medjugorje with me before he passed away. He had cancer and I was telling him about the power of prayer. I went down to him one day and took him out for lunch and we listened to tapes from Fr Aidan Carroll about the Eucharist and other things like the Divine Mercy. I believe my friend died in a state of grace as he made his confession and had visited Medjugorje.

I have met most of the visionaries but my favourite would be Vicka.

I had a friend when I lived in Clontarf and my daughter would pal around with his daughter; his wife died very suddenly a few years ago and my own daughter rang me from Australia and asked me would I bring my neighbour over to Medjugorje as he was feeling lonely and depressed after the loss of his wife. I asked him would he like to go and he agreed. He had a fantastic week. At the time he had a large mole on his forehead and he had received a letter from a consultant stating that he would need to have it investigated when he came home from his trip as it could be cancerous.

My wife knew Vicka well and we went to her house where the visionary laid her hands on both my wife and my friend and said healing prayers. On the way home in the airport we were in the bar and my friend asked me if I noticed anything strange about him. I didn't know what he meant until he asked me to look at his forehead and I noticed that the large mole had totally disappeared.

Vicka also laid her hands on me for healing prayers and every time I go to Medjugorje I also love to listen to her talk from the steps.

While in Medjugorje back in 2006, I was sitting in Colombo's having a coffee and I met a very spiritual lady and we began talking. I told her that I was with the Legion of Mary and I was going around spreading the word of the gospel to people but I was also opening my shops on a Sunday and I knew that I was committing a sin.

When you get close to God and Our Blessed Lady you know when you are doing wrong and when you are committing a sin. You know in your heart and soul that you can't hide what you are doing. I knew what I was doing was wrong but I was trying to brush it under the carpet. My whole Sunday seemed to be built around my work, while my wife was at home with my children and grandchildren. I could see the sad faces when I was going into work on a Sunday afternoon and I could see the young men who worked for me also leaving their families for the day and I wasn't happy with it all.

While speaking to this girl in Colombo's I told her that I was thinking of closing the business on Sundays. She jumped up and kissed me and told me that this was wonderful and the right thing to do. She gave me literature from America and encouraged me by saying that I would get many gifts back from God, even though I may lose money by doing this. She told me these gifts would outshine the money.

In 2008 I decided to close the doors of my businesses on Sundays. It didn't suit everyone at the time but I feel now that the staff have their Sundays back to spend with their families. I prayed to God about it and wanted to give just one day a week back to him as it is a special day and the Sabbath day. I got close to God by doing this and closer to my religion. Now on a Sunday, I get up and visit the graveyard and I look forward to going to Mass. I help out at the Morning Star and then maybe go back to the church in the afternoon for Adoration. I completely relax and chill out.

I met a lovely woman called Nuala Byrne, who was in her nineties, through the Legion of Mary. She raised a big family and all her children did very well for themselves. She told me that she 'never washed a nappy on a Sunday' and gave her whole day to God. She told me that she was glad I had closed my doors on a Sunday but that God's doors were always open. This really inspired me and I am much happier in myself because of it.

What does Medjugorje mean to me?

When I started out in business over thirty years ago, I used to go down to Moone Abbey for a few days to chill out and get away from everything. Now I go to Medjugorje and find it to be a most special place; so special that I find it hard to describe. There is so much peace and I forget my troubles, my business and my woes when I am there. It is a place where you can pass your worries over to Jesus. I adore it and love it and if I went out of business tomorrow I would be living out there.

It is the nearest thing to heaven in this life.

Ivan, Jakov and Ivanka during an apparition back in the early days.

Louise outside St James Church for the 30th anniversary of the apparitions.

Blue Cross

Maureen Maher and her daughter Nicky
who inspired her to travel to Medjugorje

The Irish flag flies high amidst the crowds on the Feast of Corpus Christi.

From left to right: Mirjana, Ivanka, her husband and Vicka

Hrvoje Joe Topić

Left: The cross in the sky was clearly visible to many on 15 August 2012 as pilgrims and locals celebrated the Feast of the Assumption.

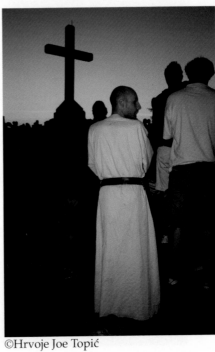

©Hrvoje Joe Topić

Mount Križevac

Louise and Ivan.

Left: The statue of Our Lady inside St James Church.

Above: Des Kelly climbing Križevac

©Hrvoje Joe Topić

The Risen Christ statue, situated behind St James Church.

A young girl carries a lighted candle during a procession on the streets of Medjugorje.

from left to right: Tom Mullins, Jackie 'The Farmer' O'Sullivan and Denis Dineen

©Hrvoje Joe Topić

The white statue of Our Lady lit up at night on Apparition Hill.

Left: St James Church lit up night for the 30th anniversa of the apparitions.

Right: Maria giving a talk in the Dome at the back of the church.

Left: A group of young people light candles during a ceremony.

Louise with a group of pilgrims outside St James Church
during the trip in 2011.

Charlie Lennon (*front left*) and fellow pilgrims enjoy
a meal in a local restaurant in Medjugorje.

Maureen, Vicka and Louise
the Green Room in RTÉ wh
Vicka appeared on *The Lat*
Late Show in February 2011

Vicka at the RDS, Dublin, during
her visit to Ireland in 2011.

©Una Williams

Fr Svet celebrates Holy Mass in St James Church on the day
of the 30th anniversary of the apparitions.

15

Jason Hamilton

Jason Hamilton was born into a Unionist and Church of Ireland family. As a young man he became very ill and was at one stage suicidal. However, after feeling a 'Fatherly presence' during one of his darkest moments, Jason redis-covered his faith, yet was still somewhat troubled as to which religion was for him. A chance meeting with a priest at a Youth Festival in Medjugorje solved this dilemma.

This is Jason's testimony.

Having been born into a Unionist and Church of Ireland family in Portadown, Co. Armagh, just before the outbreak of the Troubles, my Protestant credentials were pretty good. Even the feast day for my name, Jason, is 12 July – the day that victory over the Papist King James is celebrated in Northern Ireland.

So where did it all go wrong?

Despite a loving family, great neighbours and thoroughly enjoying much of my life, by the time I was seventeen, like so many other young men, I was troubled by 'dark clouds' of uncertainty that threatened my youthful enthusiasm.

If everything was so good, why did I often feel so painfully empty inside? Keen to escape the life-zapping heaviness of sectarianism (and Christian hypocrisy) that, to my mind, pervaded everything from school to the disco, I packed my bags for the mainland (England) to do a degree … and to party!

After a year of such living, I became ill. At first I thought I would be able to fight it out and quickly recover, but, alas, the damage was too deep. Before long, devoid of all the pleasures I had held so dear, I was back home in Northern Ireland, face-to-face with my own pain and misery and with the diagnosis of a long-term debilitating illness.

Needless to say, my thoughts soon turned to despair, with the temp-tation to commit suicide growing more and more attractive, until after one particularly painful day I decided to end it all.

By the grace of God, I didn't go through with it, sobered only by a vague sense that perhaps some greater pain awaited me 'on the other side' if I went through with it.

Around the same time, a welcome fatherly presence made itself felt as I lay on my bed of torment. A soft, gentle breeze of promise and hope grew stronger until the dam of tears burst inside me. (No doubt the fruit of my parent's prayers and other good souls who were trying to reach out to me.)

Despite being quite bitter at the hand I felt I had been dealt in life, I uttered my first prayers in many years. As I pondered and prayed, this sense of the Father's love grew and grew, encouraging me to keep searching and hoping. Even now I can still remember so clearly that overwhelming sense of being completely loved by my new friend and Father. While I was still quite weak and ill, hope once again awakened in me, encouraged by several 'experiences' in which God guided me firmly back onto the narrow yet beautiful road of life.

Back at college I gained my degree (a miracle!) and was now faced – as a young believer – with the confusing choice of which church I should attend. Having already suffered so much for my wrong choices in life, I felt it was important to discern this one wisely. Besides, it was only common sense to me, that one of Christ's churches must have it right!

As many can testify after recovering from an illness, even a heavy flu, there is often a unique clarity of thought which follows. In my case this 'clarity' helped me greatly as I tried various denominations of Christian worship. Needless to say, my open-mindedness ended at the doors of the Catholic Church, which any self-respecting, Bible-believing Christian could tell you was just plain wrong.

After several months of praying, questioning, studying and searching, I reached a point where I could honestly say, 'Okay Lord, I've searched but I haven't found your church, so now, it's over to you. I don't care what it costs, I just want the truth!'

As G. K. Chesterton once said: 'Keep an open mind, but not so open that your brains fall out!'

The Lord showed me that I needed to humble myself and pray more.

To cut a long story short, I was invited by a tough old Irish nun to come to Medjugorje for a youth festival in 1991. Once there, I walked around in an uncomfortable daze, revolted by all the jangling beads and Catholicism, yet touched by the obvious transformation and joy on so many faces.

After a few days I decided to 'bite the bullet' and speak to someone. That someone happened to be a joyful and wise American priest. The conversation went something like this: 'Here, how's it going? I'm not actually a Catholic but I was wondering if you could listen and help me repent as I want to be a better Christian?' (Prods, eh?) I mentioned nothing of my hidden quest.

As I was reading my list, the Lord (helped by this wise priest) opened my mind about two things: firstly he showed me that what I was looking for wasn't so much the 'True Church' but love; unconditional and complete love.

He showed me that this love is to be found most fully in Holy Communion with the Person of Jesus Christ in the blessed sacrament. Secondly (God doesn't play fair sometimes), he showed me that the blessed sacrament is at the heart of and can only be found in the Catholic Church. Moreover, he showed me that this is his Church – not made by man but perfect in every way (marred only by human sinfulness). I decided that yes, my search was over.

Many years later, I am often moved to tears of gratitude when I recall the incredible blessings the Lord has showered on me, despite my waywardness and unfaithfulness. I have come to know Jesus as my best friend, Saviour, Brother and Love; although I find one of the joys of our faith is the sense that with God the best is always yet to come. While life can be hard and sometimes unbearable, Jesus has given us the most intimate part of himself (within the Catholic Church) to strengthen us for these trials and make us whole! 'The glory of God is man fully alive,' as St Irenaeus once said. Moreover (and this never ceases to amaze me), he has given us his own Mother to be there for poor unfortunates like myself, and to bring us all to the joys of heaven – often despite ourselves. God is good.

What does Medjugorje mean to me?

Medjugorje was the key to my whole conversion and I feel it is an extraordinary place for those who are searching for God – a portal of heaven. I am eternally grateful that Our Blessed Mother cast her eyes down on a wretch like me and saw the man I could become. As the psalmist says: 'How can I repay the Lord for the things that he has done for me?'

16

Josephine McGroarty

Josephine McGroarty was immediately concerned when her son returned from a village where Our Lady was supposedly appearing. Alarmed by his enthusiasm, and that of his peers, she made a decision to go over and expose the village for what it really was. However, what started off as a mission to discredit the happenings in Medjugorje turned into an experience that saw the mother of eight return to the village over forty times.

This is Josephine's testimony.

My name is Josephine and I come from North Donegal. I was married to my husband Jim for forty-one years. He died suddenly two and a half years ago. We have been blessed with eight children and eight grandchildren. When I was asked to write this article, I felt unsure. Thoughts of my dear husband came to mind. He had travelled to Medjugorje forty-four times. I write this in his memory. I hope you enjoy my recollections of the earlier days.

Let me tell you how my trip to Medjugorje came about.

We had promised our children a foreign trip if they worked hard in the Junior Certificate. Our eldest daughter, Sally Marie, performed well in her exams and so travelled to Switzerland in 1986. Next it was our son's turn to avail of the reward in 1987, but, alas, he returned from school one day distraught. His planned tour to Holland had been cancelled. Loreto Colleges had cancelled school trips as a result of a tragedy involving a teacher and a student in Devonshire. That cancelled trip was to have a profound effect on our family in the years to come.

As a consolation for Liam's disappointment I had planned for him to travel with my sister to Liverpool in August. However, fate intervened. My friend, Mary, told me of an available seat on a foreign trip with Youth for Peace, which was due to depart from Knock in two days.

Since Liam was never away from home before, I was naturally concerned. I did not know the name of the planned destination. I could not pronounce it. I asked many questions and was re-assured that a priest, a teacher and a group leader would be with the group, therefore it would be well supervised. Mary's three children, who were older than Liam, were travelling. I agreed.

When Liam returned from school he was so excited when I told him the news. Time passed quickly. Liam promised to ring on arrival. After two days of no contact I was really anxious. I rang Mary. She told me that I would have no word because there were no phones there.

'The place is very primitive,' she told me, 'You do know,' she said, 'Our Lady is supposed to be appearing there.'

If I had been aware of this I would not have allowed my son to go. I was annoyed. I always performed my Catholic duties; pilgrimages, however, were not my scene.

Something crossed my mind; I recalled an article from the *Sunday World* a few years earlier called 'Is the Sun Really Spinning in a Yugoslavian Village?'

I remember reading briefly through it and smiling to myself, thinking how the media create sensational stories to sell papers. Surely this could not be where they have taken our son. Time past slowly.

The bus returned and Liam was home. He looked so well. He was full of joy and enthusiasm. He was eager to tell all he had witnessed. The other youths were the same. It was lovely to see all of them full of joy, excitement and awe as they relayed their experiences. However, I had my doubts.

Liam wanted somebody from our house to go. He wanted one of us to share his experience. Despite my reluctance and unease, I made my plan to go and check it out. I had to see what was causing this 'stir' and expose it. These Youth for Peace trips were questionable in my opinion. Any strange activity would have to be uncovered. I would equip myself with notepaper. I would record my findings.

I was given the list of necessities to bring, such as crackers, cheese, crisps, chocolate, drinks, tea bags, powdered milk, jungle spray and toilet paper, among other things. I remember packing a box of Black Magic chocolates. As the time of departure drew near I was afraid.

What would I find? What would I do if I found evidence to support my suspicions? Protecting the youths was important to me. This 'apparition' tale had to be exposed. The many words of advice were echoing in my ears, especially Liam's warning never to be alone. I had two big cases, one filled with clothes and toiletries and the other with food. With thoughts such as these, I made my first trip to Medjugorje.

The bus left from Letterkenny for Knock at 3.30 a.m. It was a long tiring journey. So many thoughts crowded my mind. Thoughts of foolishness, whether I was crazy to be embarking on this journey, exhaustion, anxiety, fear of travel and homesickness. A Donegal priest brought us quickly from our slumber as the Joyful Mysteries were recited. I recall a young person praying for his diseased brother at the third mystery. We got to Knock and a little voice in my head whispered: 'What is wrong with you Josephine?'

Knock

As the plane rushed along on the tarmac, tears ran down my face. I was frightened. Fear of the unknown. The only comfort I had were the lovely blessed rosary beads that Liam had given me. Ivan, the visionary, had given the Irish youths rosary beads before they departed for home. Liam advised me to wear them at all times. I had them around my neck. I held on to these beads when the flight was taking off. Anyone who knows me or has travelled with me knows that my behaviour is anything but normal when I hear my flight being called. The name of the aircraft was *Queen of Peace*, which was some consolation.

Mostar Airport

Mostar was a military airport. I was sure the plane would hit the mountain as it had to veer its way inside a long, narrow, hilly terrain. After a long turbulent flight, we arrived at 11.50 a.m. A big blonde female security officer who, as many of you who have been there will remember, was austere greeted us. My packed food case drew her attention. My husband had tied special cord on it to prevent it bursting. I suggested she use a knife to cut the cords. 'No *comprehendo*,' was her reply. She could see my fear and relented. The customs and passport inspection was equally unpleasant. If I was waiting for a *céad míle fáilte* it was absent in these faces of hostility. There were no toilets in the airport. There was a hole in the ground. I knew to be patient. This was an unsafe place. The military atmosphere was threatening. We were taken into what an area that was like a cattle pen. We were forbidden from communicating with the departing pilgrims nearby.

Bus journey

We were transferred to Medjugorje in a noisy bus, through rocky hills and winding roads. Sandra was the guide. Her broken English brought little comfort to me. I was hungry and lonesome. I wondered what might have been Liam's impression at this stage of his trip. I put my hand to my neck and was pleased the rosary beads had survived the Mostar Airport ordeal. Sandra told us, 'You were sent for. Our Lady called each of you here.' Alarm bells! Was this the start of the brainwashing? I thought to myself that nobody would possibly have come here voluntarily.

Medjugorje

We arrived in Medjugorje. Everything here was 'go slow'. Even the animals grazed silently. The sheep and goats wore bells around their necks. There was eeriness in the stillness. Even the sound of the breeze mirrored the creepiness. We were brought to the wrong house – no room at the inn. Nothing was going to plan, if indeed there ever was a plan. We were finally brought to a third house. A small tractor took our cases to our destination. The road was too bad for the bus. We followed on foot behind the tractor. The potholes were like craters. The place was so barren. The poverty unreal. After a long walk, we arrived at Antone's house. We were introduced to his family. I heard Owen, Nicola, Sheams, Statea, Sivetze, Statco, Ostojic Andelko, Bijakavici, Ivana, Iva. Will I ever remember any of these names? I'll just record.

Finally settled in our new abode, I shared a room with Kathleen. To say the accommodation was basic was an understatement. We were told to go straight to the chapel. We walked for twenty minutes. The Croatian service lasted for over three hours. After about fifteen decades of rosary, dying with hunger, cold and boredom, I asked myself again what had brought me here. I wanted to go home.

Back to our host family. The food was poor and I could not get a phone to ring Jim. The host family tried to make us welcome. Old Antone sang what sounded like a rebel song. I wished I knew their language, 'No Problems' seemed to be the only phrase they knew. We noticed earlier that Antone did not wear shoes. He had an injured foot. Apparently, when he was young he got caught in a trap on the mountain. His family had a newborn baby and we were given christening cake for our 'tea'.

A nice nurse, Ann, from Letterkenny, stayed in our house. She was returning home the following day, having facilitated the airlines by spending extra time due to overbooking. Ann was very consoling when I expressed my complaints. Suddenly, I felt trapped. I felt an urgency to escape. Since Ann was so happy here, and had opted to stay extra time, it seemed reasonable for me to swap places with her and head home. I suggested as much to her. Her joyful response was, 'I felt just like you do, but it will grow on you.'

I replied, 'I don't think I'll stay here long enough for it to grow on me!'

Upstairs, the chocolates had not melted. We helped ourselves. I could hear the wild animals. I went to my journal to record. I did not want to miss a bar.

We met Sandra, as agreed, under the big tree, outside the chapel. At 5.40 p.m. throngs of birds descended. I could not hear Sandra's instruction. Between her broken English, the noisy birds, the wind and dusty grime the situation was impossible. Sandra explained that these birds relocated to the tree closer to the church since the apparitions moved there. Am I interested? Not a bit.

Night One

Ready for bed after a long day, I pulled down the blankets only to see a huge insect with fangs and wings crawling where I am to sleep. I cursed silently as I took in my surroundings. It was wretched. I thought: 'If I were home I would be muttering a few prayers before bed, but here I am cursing. Maybe I should pray.' I went to my neck to get my precious rosary beads. To my horror I found the beads were gone. Kathleen said she was sure I wore them at Knock and at Mostar. I checked my clothes, emptied my cases. No luck. I went on my knees. I started to look and feel on the dark concrete floor. I could hear the howling of foxes, dogs, roosters and birds in the distance. Everything seemed to come to life. I spotted a little rusted tin which served as a bin. I looked into it and there I found my rosary beads, unbroken and intact. We offered a fervent prayer in thanksgiving. I hoped dearly that Ann, the nurse, would swap places with me in the morning. I would go home, abandon my mission and forget this plan. My detective skills were faltering.

Day Two

I got up at 5.30 a.m. I was really wishing that I could take Ann's place. However, she refused and tried to console me by saying, 'You'll need a few days to settle, everyone does. It's a thawing out process. Give it a chance.' I gave her my Jim's phone number and told her to ring him as soon as she arrived in Letterkenny. This is what you tell him: 'I will be home as soon as I can get a plane out of here. I could never stick this for a week. This is worse than Lough Derg.'

I headed to the Tour Operator's Office. I told them I had to get out immediately. The lady only stared at me. She showed me a calendar and

I was left in no doubt that the next flight would be Thursday. Six days away. I pleaded with her. 'I must get out of here.'

She replied, 'I do not *comprehendo*.' I was getting more frustrated. Take me to London, Paris, Rome, anywhere. She just smiled and this made me worse. I thought, this young lady is just pretending. I looked at her again and wondered how on earth I could get her attention.

I produced £300 sterling and pleaded with her, 'Will you take me to a beach?' I hoped this bombshell would get the desired response.

But no, she still smiled on and said, 'I do not *comprehendo*.'

I struggled through that day, attending all church activities. I watched as these birds descended again. The tree was over-laden with the birds and its branches appeared weighed down. These tiny birds, like hail-stones, arrived at speed through the air. Their chatter mysteriously stopped at 5.40 p.m. This was significant. At home, during the lambing season, the farmers often have imitation gunfire go off at intervals to ward off any foxes, etc. I thought the same might apply to these birds. Perhaps something happens on the mountain at 5.39 p.m. to disturb these tiny birds, causing them to make a fast exit from their habitat. Since I could not get out of here and with six days to fill in, I would do something useful and continue with my original plan. I would find out what was happening. I would remain vigilant.

During the second night, I could not sleep and walked outside. On returning to my room, I went to the wrong door and I saw Antone, lying on the concrete floor, no mattress, just a coat over him. I recognised his disfigured foot. I felt so hopeless. To think he gave up his bed for me. Then Sandra's words were ringing in my ears: 'Our Lady told these people that they would open their hearts and their homes to the people who would come from the four corners of the earth.'

I observed everyone and everything with suspicion. Fast Day was announced on Wednesday morning. I was up early. A big jug of water and dry bread was on the table. The water looked a bit cloudy. I decided not to drink their water or eat their food. This way I would not come under their 'spell' – were we being drugged? Drugs could easily be put in the water and with the pangs of hunger, one would not notice a taste.

I had concerns that had to be addressed. I must make sure that the truth of this 'Peace', 'Mir' or 'Gospa' tale was brought to light. I considered that it might be a ploy to gain access to revenue. I headed off. I had ample supply of coke, chocolates, crisps, sweets and, most importantly, my beloved Carroll's No. 1 tipped cigarettes. I had not partaken in any of the organised events, hence, I had no idea where anything was. My plan was to solve the bird puzzle by getting to the highest mountain and finding this 'imitation gun'.

Day Three

I headed off on my mission. At about 5.50 a.m. I was at the foot of a mountain. I saw an elderly priest; he was sitting alone on a stone. He was staring at the sky and looked as if he was praying aloud. This is what I heard:

'And when I return to Quebec and I tell my parishioners what I am now witnessing, they will tell me it's an optical illusion.'

I was drawn to look. I saw something that I will never forget. It was a private revelation between my God and me. No words could explain. Unbelievable, unexplainable and unforgettable.

I embarked on a journey deep within. A voice whispered, 'You must get to the top of that mountain.' Exhausted, I rested a while. I opened my bag of 'goodies' and as I was now very hungry, I devoured my chocolates drowned with a can of coke. Then I remembered my cigarettes. A thought came to me. I would love to get a wee sign to know this was for real. Am I hallucinating? Are the birds a figment of my imagination? I recall singing this hymn 'Come back to me with all your heart, don't let fear keep us apart ...'

Then I make the deal. 'Mary, I find it hard to believe the half of what I hear or see – if you are here and you are responsible for all of this – I won't ask for much. I have been smoking since I was thirteen years old and presently smoking about forty daily. I don't really want to ever stop, even if I could, but you take away the craving to smoke from me for *one* day and then I will believe.'

I had often tried to go off cigarettes for Lent, but when noon came on Ash Wednesday I believed I was a hero. Again on Good Friday, I considered my sacrifice complete if I lasted without smoking until midday. So with total faith in my heart, I opened my bag and removed my 20-pack of Carroll's No. 1. I lifted a stone and placed the pack underneath. I sat and smiled to myself, in awe at what I had actually done. 'Now,' I said, 'we are talking.'

I just sat there. Time held no meaning. I then just wandered about. Suddenly, I realised I was lost. I was going around in circles. There did not appear to be a summit. There I remained, wandering around trying to find my bearings. I was terrified. I became aware of many living creatures, such as reptiles and crawly minute snake-like objects. What was I to do? I fell to my knees helplessly. Something strange happened.

I was suddenly taken back in time to my home place in Donegal; to when I was eight or nine years old. I was beside a huge cliff adjacent to the Lighthouse. Our animals had broken out and had wandered to the cliff and my sister was trying to get these animals back to safety. We had this little animal that we petted as a calf. As he got older, he would playfully dunt you with his horns. My sister was trying to rescue these animals from the Cliffside with a little *buachalán buí*. I had visions of the calf dunting my sister and knocking her out over the cliff, which was overhanging the big swell of a rough sea.

I was back in that very spot, feeling the pain, hopelessness, anguish and fear for her life. I don't know for how long this experience lasted. It was heart-wrenching. Then this peace descended upon me, something I had never known existed. I felt like someone had placed an umbrella over my head and my whole body was secure and at peace in this tent-like enclosure. Nothing could harm me now. Something was caring for me and cradling me from the dangers of the outside world.

Very soon another episode flashed through my mind. It was my early days at school. I saw this burn (stream) and the water was very high. My older sister had to lift me by the waist and throw me across this burn. I felt the terror of not landing safely on the other side of the deep stream. Again, these feelings of fear and uncertainty overpowered me. I sat and relived the pain and fear, secure in the knowledge that I was safe and being looked after while I stayed in this Oasis. Nothing could break this peace or take it away. I was totally dependent on this power.

Many other traumatic memories from my past surfaced. I relived and felt the pain of each one of them. In some strange way, I can now only remember the joy of those precious moments or hours. Something within me had changed forever. Afterward, I recall, I did not even feel the sun, as this invisible umbrella was my shelter and protection.

Suddenly I was brought back to reality thinking: 'Now you are here alone. You are lost. It is dark. You are far from home. You are not afraid. No one knows where you are.' It was 28 September 1987. I was on the mountain since before 6 a.m. Suddenly, I heard the sound of music coming up from the valley. Is this a heavenly choir? I decided to follow the choir. I had no torch or coat. It was so very dark. I don't know how, but I arrived down at the chapel following the sound of the music. I met James. He seemed annoyed with me. He asked where I had been and I simply replied that I could not speak. 'That's a terrible thing you have done. People were looking for you,' he said. I had totally forgotten that I had gone to the tour operator's office, where they had recalled that a distressed pilgrim intended to get an urgent flight out of the country.

Day Four

I slept soundly. I awakened to the sound of many wild animals and cocks crowing. But far from being a frightening sound it was a call inviting me to come away to a lonely place where I could be alone and rest awhile. I returned to the mountain, which I now knew to be Podbrdo or Apparition Hill. I sat down. I said some prayers. I took out a new pack of cigarettes. I said, 'Thanks, Mary, I know you are here. I believe now. Send back the craving now and in gratitude and penance I will offer up the pangs of withdrawal myself for this day.' I can in truth say that from that minute until this present day, I have never known the craving for nicotine.

Days Five and Six

Heaven on earth. Why do I have to go home?

Conclusion

After thirty-nine trips, there are many amazing things that I could write about, for example: Jim and myself renewing our Ruby Wedding vows; our special meetings with Vicka; special time with family members and especially the precious memory in St James Church where our son, Fr Damian, offered Holy Mass shortly after his dad's death; precious moments at the Blue Cross with Paul and family singing *Faith of Our Fathers*; the locals giving me a few grapes along the way as I tramp through their fields; the man Siobhan and I met on the mountain in the dark of night giving me a red rose; dew drops falling out of clear moonlit sky; Frances and I on Podbrdo; and the many pilgrims who have journeyed there with me over the years, each of them have inspired me with their faith and courage. The camaraderie and the joy one experiences there is unbelievable. The peace, the laughter, the tears, the wonder and awe in God's presence. Oftentimes, I ponder in my heart and reflect where my life would have led me if I had not found Medjugorje almost twenty-five years ago. What a glorious blessing for our family.

The cancellation of Liam's trip from Loreto Convent, Milford heralded my trip to Medjugorje. Our Lady had plans in place. She beckoned me to her son in that Oasis of Peace, stretched out her hand and whispered, 'Thanks for responding to my call.'

17

Kevin Cunningham

The loss of Kevin Cunningham's father at a young age had a massive impact on him and his family. Losing his brother, who was only twenty-five years of age, tragically, some years later threw more devastation into Kevin's life. Kevin's first impression's of Medjugorje after his father's death left him feeling lost and asking the question, 'Does God know me?' Returning to the village many years later helped him come to terms with his younger brother's untimely death.

This is Kevin's testimony.

My father Martin was tragically killed on 7 October 1987, on the Feast of the Holy Rosary. He was just forty-three years of age and left a young wife and five children behind, ranging from thirteen to nineteen years of age. This had a massive impact on all our lives, which had been centred around Mass, the family rosary and a great love of hurling. It was hugely important to my mother and father that we all got down on our knees each night to pray the rosary. The night before my father died just after we had finished praying the rosary I passed by his room and saw him down on his knees praying at his bedside. This remains a lasting memory of my father.

It was very hard to cope with his death and especially difficult for my mother having to manage four teenage boys and a young daughter, particularly growing up during the time of the Troubles. My mother had to be both mother and father to us and I could see the strain of this, especially those times when I caught a glimpse of her tearful eyes.

It was in 1989 that my mother first heard about Medjugorje from a friend. There was a video about Medjugorje that was meant to be shown in our local parochial hall after the Novena Mass but the video didn't work and the priest got up and began talking to us about Medjugorje instead. I was fascinated by what he had to say about these six young children and the village he described. He spoke so highly about Medjugorje that I thought if what he said was true and that these children really were having daily visitations from Our Lady then I had to see this place for myself.

Around the same time, my uncle had been released from prison. He was a political prisoner and, not having had my father around, I probably looked up to him. My cousin and I used to hang around with him and as an impressionable young lad I could easily have been influenced by his political beliefs which could have led me down a completely different path.

After the talk in the parochial hall, my mother invited me, my brother Sean and my sister Deborah to go to Medjugorje in April of 1990. To me, it was an opportunity to go and see this place for myself, in a worst case scenario it would be a foreign holiday away for a week in the sun. Off we went to Medjugorje; and when we arrived it was teeming rain! The mud was flowing down the streets and it was a murky looking place, so my first impressions were not great. I went to bed and got up the next morning and went to Mass.

I was expecting to see things in the sky as I had been listening to people talking about this, that and the other. However, it wasn't what I had expected at all. To keep my mother happy, I would go to Mass then I would disappear, going back to the house we were staying in, getting into bed and pulling the covers over my head. The rain was relentless.

Both my brother and sister were actively participating, but not me. I remember one day in particular, I was extremely bored so I went for a walk down the street when I heard singing. I went around to the Dome at the back of the church and I saw my brother singing in the middle of this crowd of young people. I shook my head and walked away feeling embarrassed. This was alien to me.

There was a big, burly man staying in our house, he was a building contractor. I sat and talked with him one day at length and he explained that while Medjugorje may be a nice place, it wasn't for him. He and his wife had lost a child and he felt that his wife was getting a lot out of being in Medjugorje and so, like me, he was going along with it. However we both agreed that it wasn't really for either of us.

Later on that week, I was sitting having a coffee and this same man and his wife walked up to me. The rain had disappeared and it was a beautiful evening with a clear blue sky. He had this expression on his face and he turned to me and said, 'Kevin, be here in two minutes. I want to have a chat with you.' I instantly knew there was something up. He sat down at the table beside me and said, 'I have been sitting with you all week, slagging this place off and talking about all the lunatics that are out here.' He told me how he was standing at the side of the chapel at around the same time Our Lady was appearing and he heard a group of children creating a bit of a commotion. He looked over at them and saw them looking up at the sky. 'I saw a luminous cross suspended in the sky. I can't deny what I've seen with my own eyes,' he told me.

As he was talking, I could see tears coming down his face. At that moment, although I believed him, I felt very alone and felt like my trusted friend had gone – I was now on my own. I asked myself the question, 'Does God know me?'

I don't know why but, all of a sudden, I felt the urge to go to confession. At home, I would have gone to confession out of obligation as it was the 'done thing' but with hindsight I really didn't understand the significance of the sacrament. While walking down the street towards the church, I heard music and saw a man whom I had seen earlier in the week exclaiming, 'Jesus loves you, Jesus loves you,' in a broad Belfast accent. I thought to myself that he wouldn't be running around the streets of Belfast saying that! I really wasn't into all that sort of thing but I did stop and listened to him as he began to give his testimony.

He talked about how he was guard of honour at Bobby Sands' funeral and of his experiences as a member of the IRA growing up in West Belfast and the story of his conversion swapping 'bullets for beads'. I was intrigued by all this as some people I knew had been heavily involved in the Troubles. After listening to him, my first impression had very quickly changed.

I went to confession and said to the priest, 'Father, I believe this place to be a holy place but I really feel that God does not know me.'

He took me by the hand and said, 'Where two or more are gathered in my name, there am I in their midst.' He pointed at himself, he pointed at me and he pointed upwards. To this day, I do not know exactly what happened to me but it was some sort of spiritual awakening. I felt that my soul had been cleansed, something had replaced the void within me, and for the first time I truly felt God's presence and experienced an immense peace. That feeling remained with me for the rest of the week.

When I boarded the plane to go home, a woman said to me, 'I can see you got a lot out of Medjugorje. I can see the peace in your eyes.' I had been going out with a girl back home and just felt like I couldn't be with her anymore because of the experience I had. I saw things differently. When I returned she told me that she couldn't look at me, that there was something different about my eyes. She also could see something had changed in me.

I returned to Medjugorje in July of that year with my other brothers, Martin and Pat, who were going for the first time along with a group of young people who had seen what the place had done for me and the rest of my family. They wanted to visit this place for themselves. They too were very impressed, each one returning home having had their own personal experience of grace and inner peace. At this point, my family started a Medjugorje prayer group within the home, as had been requested by Our Lady through one of the visionaries. After I came home, a work colleague who was a born again Christian began to challenge me about my faith and about God. He was a very nice man but was totally convinced that all Roman Catholics were destined for hell. My foundation had been rocked. I was at a point where I nearly lost my faith. I began to doubt where my father had gone after his passing and was really struggling for the first time since my return from Medjugorje. Up until this point, I had been going to prayer groups during the week and to Mass, Adoration and the rosary every Friday night with my mother and other family members and friends. However, I was also saying to myself during this time of struggle that I didn't want to face God if the born again Christian was right and I was wrong. This struggle continued for a period of many months.

A friend of mine who knew I was struggling and questioning my faith came to me and said, 'Kevin, I have a tape for you about a Protestant minister who converts to Catholicism.' (*The Conversion of Scott Hahn*) I listened carefully to the tape and was amazed that it answered most of the questions that I had been challenged on concerning Catholic theology. For me, it was a godsend. So I completely immersed myself in learning all about my faith. I was able to return to the born again Christian who had challenged me. It turned out that not only was I now in a position to defend my faith but I left him with unanswered questions. As one great theologian said, 'The Catholic Church is like a caged lion, just let it out and it will defend itself.'

The war broke out in Yugoslavia in 1991 and we were unable to travel back to Medjugorje for a few years. It was this same year that I would meet my future wife and we continued to actively participate in church life and Medjugorje prayer groups.

I married Andrea in March 1994 and we went to Medjugorje in July of that same year, offering up our prayers in the hope of starting a family. Having been blessed with daughters, Margaret born in 1995 and Kerry in 1996, it was a couple of years before I returned to Medjugorje again.

Then, tragedy struck my family for the second time, a devastating blow. On 2 August 1997, my youngest brother, Pat, was killed in a hit-and-run accident while living in the States. It was the Feast Day of Our Lady of the Angels.

My life fell apart and I simply couldn't cope with the loss of my brother. Pat and I were very close and the morning I saw him leave for the States, I said to my wife that I knew I would never see him again. She thought I was just upset and sentimental but I felt it in my heart. Pat left with the intention of going to America for one year. He left on 11 February 1997, the Feast Day of Our Lady of Lourdes.

For the following year, I found it impossible to communicate with or be around the people I loved. I had so much anger within me and so many unanswered questions about my brother's death. I asked God why my family had to suffer another devastating loss, why my mother, having lost a husband, had now lost a son and my siblings and I, having lost a father, now had lost our cherished brother. I was becoming more and more disillusioned with life as each day passed. I found it difficult to talk to my wife about the loss of my brother Pat as she also had been very close to him. It was just too difficult for us to talk to each other about him. My wife would later describe how painful it was for her to watch the person she loved slowly slip away from family life, from God, from life itself and she felt powerless to do anything about it. It was during this time that the local priest, who was around the same age as myself, continued to visit our home offering words of advice, support and friendship. It seemed easier to talk to someone who didn't know Pat. It didn't take away from the pain but Father Peter was just the person I needed at that time – don't get me wrong, often times he told me it exactly like it was, he was straight-talking and somehow managed to challenge, guide and support me during the most difficult period of my life and would somehow appear at just the appropriate moment. My wife called him my 'Second Guardian Angel' as it would happen that just when I was at breaking point and simply unable to cope with the loss I felt, he would walk through the front door.

One day, my oldest brother, Martin, asked me what I thought about getting away to Medjugorje for a week. I looked at him and said, 'Go there – are you for real?' It seemed to me that the closer I got to God, the more struggles and heartaches I had. My mother was worried at how affected I had been by Pat's death and suggested to my wife that she would like to send my brother and me to Medjugorje. It was the last place on earth we wanted to go to.

At this point, it was a welcome relief to my wife such was her own desperation, watching her husband simply existing, not living life anymore. Having to cope with the demands of two young children was certainly too exhausting for someone who was barely functioning, not eating and not sleeping properly. I remember once being out in the hallway in the months after my brother's death and just collapsing to the floor. My two-year-old daughter had her arms outstretched to me but I was so consumed with grief I couldn't even hold her.

My brother Pat was the youngest boy in the house and only twenty-five at the time of his death, he was so full of life and a real character. Everyone knew Pat, he was a great hurler, a great athlete, a real joker and no one could believe something like this had happened to someone like him, someone so full of life.

After a lot of debating, both my brother Martin and I reluctantly went to Medjugorje. I remember sitting on the bus on the way from the airport to Medjugorje and there were two people sitting in front of us talking about God and peace and prayer. We both wanted to get off the bus at that point. We really didn't want to be in their company for a whole week. Ironically, Martin and I ended up sharing the same room as one of them and during the course of the week we shared many hearty laughs with him.

My brother Martin urged me to go and see Philip Ryan who worked as a guide in the village. Philip knew Pat and had heard about his death. He said to me, 'Kevin, take yourself up to the big mountain and leave all your anger in front of the Cross.' I walked across the fields through the vineyards and climbed Mount Križevac. The tears were welling up in my eyes and before long I could not stop crying. It was the first sense of release since Pat's death. Martin and I spent a lot of time on our own, sharing breakfast together and then going our separate ways searching for something – answers, consolation, peace – anything that would relieve the pain and suffering of our loss.

Later that week, my brother and I were sitting on the steps of the old graveyard behind St James Church under the shadow of Mount Križevac talking about Daddy and Pat and reliving our childhood memories. I really felt like I needed Pat to appear to me and tell me that he was fine in order for me to get the comfort I desired. I wanted him to let me know he was OK so that I could get on with my life.

Suddenly, the picture came into my mind of that day when I saw my eldest daughter, Margaret, putting her arms out to me and I saw myself collapsing to the floor. A great sense of guilt and regret came over me and I turned to Martin and said, 'I haven't been a good husband or a good father since Pat's death.'

I had come to Medjugorje to find out if my brother was alright and here I was sitting on the steps of a graveyard realising for the first time that I hadn't been there for my wife or my children. Afterward I questioned if this was Pat telling me that I ought to take care of my family and wondered if he was reminding me of the need to take care of his little God-daughter Margaret.

When we arrived home to Dublin airport, my wife, Andrea, and my sister-in-law, Lucia, were waiting for us. As soon as Andrea saw me she smiled and said, 'Kevin, I'm glad to have you back.' I told her I was glad to be home too and she replied, 'No, I am glad to have *you* back.' She immediately knew there had been a change within me, she had seen it in my eyes. We had only talked on the phone once during the week apart and she had no indication of how the week in Medjugorje had gone for me. I have no doubt that I received great healing and a renewed sense of peace through the intercession of Our Lady of Medjugorje.

My brother Martin then decided because of all the graces that we had received from Medjugorje that he would like to start taking groups out to Medjugorje on pilgrimage, in thanksgiving. Since then, Martin and his wife Lucia have organised a yearly pilgrimage to Medjugorje from our local parish.

On one of these recent pilgrimages my friend, my daughter and I had just come from Ivan's apparition with Our Lady on Podbrdo and on the way back through the fields my friend pointed to the sky. It was a very starry night and in the sky it looked like there were a circle of flickering stars which were shimmering really bright. We continued on our way back towards the village and came across lots of people down on their knees. My friend asked me what it was but I told him that I had never seen anything like it before and I didn't know. I then asked one of the pilgrims who had been kneeling down what it was? He said to me, 'That's Our Lady's crown.' I knew there was something unusual about it but wasn't sure what. In the next moment, a bolt of lightening appeared and hit the centre of the circle of lights. It hit it once, then twice and on the third time it sucked all the shimmering lights into the bolt and it was gone.

What does Medjugorje mean to me?

I have been to Medjugorje sixteen times. Medjugorje has had an extremely positive impact on my life and on the lives of my immediate family and friends. People that I would never have associated myself with, are now some of my best buddies and I believe that Our Lady has called each one of us to Medjugorje. The experience I had during that confession on my first visit to Medjugorje was the moment I truly believed that God existed. I could have died there and then and I would not have had any fear in facing my maker.

I described my feelings about my experience of Medjugorje to a priest once and he likened it to going into the desert. He explained that in the desert of life God invites us to drink from the oasis of the living water that he has provided for us. Once you have tasted it, your thirst is quenched, you become refreshed and renewed and you will want to go back for more. Medjugorje is spoken about every single day of my life. It's not just a place, it's a way of life. After tragically losing our father and then our brother, Medjugorje has brought my family closer to God. It is hard for me to think of life without Medjugorje. I am thankful that my mother took us to Medjugorje all those years ago and that my own children, Margaret, Kerry, Laura, Kevin-Patrick and Conor, have all been able to experience the fruits of Medjugorje, a little piece of heaven on earth.

18

Donna McGettigan-Ostojić

Donna is originally from Letterkenny but went out to Medjugorje as a young girl in her twenties to work as a guide. Donna married her husband Marinko and continued to live in the village even throughout the Bosnian War. Their business Paddy Travel helps thousands of tourists with accommodation and travel arrangements. The married couple have eight children together.

This is Donna's testimony.

The last time I asked myself the question, 'What does Medjugorje mean to me?' was in 2008. It was the twentieth anniversary of my move from Letterkenny town to the village of Medjugorje, ex-Yugoslavia, and when I sat down to really think about it I ended up writing a book. After twenty years most people would have a lot to say about the place they live in – but a book!

Yes, Medjugorje called me in back in the mid-eighties, or should I say hauled me in. I came, like most Irish pilgrims back then, as part of a group, totally curious and prepared to spend the week in the 'back of beyond'. Well, to be honest that's exactly what it was like back then. Even to the most modest of Irish, we were slumming it for the week. Placed three miles from the church, separated from my friends, in a room with two grannies and not a shop or a bar in sight, this should have been the trip from hell for the 25-year-old fun-loving lass that I was.

Not so. It changed my life forever.

After a few days, and despite my reluctance to enter the pilgrimage mode, even I had to admit that something was going down, or should I say coming down. Standing before us were a group of sincere and humble kids claiming themselves as visionaries of the Blessed Mother of God. Well, to do this back then in a Communist regime you would want to be mad or under the influence of a 'lose all sense of reality drug' – both proven not to be the case. So one had to ask oneself why would these kids put themselves and their individual families in such heat with the regime, bring the army into their little village, get themselves followed, arrested, and interrogated, put their parish priest in prison and basically for many years ruin the lives of their humble neighbours? No, they didn't have a death wish and I was to realise that by the end of the week.

It was approximately in the middle of our stay when we decided to make a night trip to the larger of the two mountains, Križevac. As we stumbled upwards in the dark of night with only the light of our cheap torches to guide us, I noticed I was in the company of accountants and teachers, our leader himself a successful barrister. I distinctly remember smiling inwardly at the thought of our pupils and customers seeing us now. But on we went in determined haste. I kept my doubts about our certifiable actions to myself and answered our prayers as loudly as the next.

Some hours later we reached our destination at the foot of the large cross and well-known apparition site. We found ourselves under the stars and on top of the world, or so it seemed to us who had never seen such beauty. The prayers continued, in the silence of the night as we mumbled our replies, until eventually we lapsed into an easy silence, leaving each to his own. Some wandered into the darkness, some headed for home, others sat at the foot of the large cross to dwell upon life.

It was a night I would remember for the rest of my life and now, twenty-five years later, I still cannot find the words to describe it. To be awakened in the middle of a deep sleep could vaguely relate to the feeling that overcame me on that dark night at the foot of the large cross where the Blessed Mother had appeared many times, and where the hand of God touched this reluctant Irish pilgrim.

What do you do when like a bolt to the back of the head you are staring at the reality that the Mother of God exists and is not just a fig-urehead in my Hail Mary? I did the only thing I wanted to do back then, despite the disapproval and shock of my nearest and dearest; I gave up my job and found myself on a plane heading to Split, Yugoslavia, as a pilgrimage guide for the season 1988. I would never again question the authenticity of these apparitions, as I became overnight one of it's dedicated supporters and defenders.

Soaring temperatures, shortage of beds, old buses, and thousands of Irish pilgrims seeking the truth comes to mind when I look back on my first year as a pilgrim guide. Certainly, my four years spent in UCG and years teaching did absolutely nothing to prepare me for the dilemma of being the black box for the thousands of hot, tired, frustrated, troubled and searching pilgrims that passed through that season and the seasons to come.

But they remain and always will be the best days of my life. In the company of Claire from Limerick, Graham from Dublin, Donnacha from Athlone and Ivica from Mostar, we tended to our flocks with enthusiasm, in the hope that they would, if just for a moment, feel the same joy and privilege we felt to be in such a blessed place. Looking back I think I must have been the worst pilgrim guide ever appointed as I couldn't see past the sheer honour of doing the job and had little sympathy for those who felt the conditions were substandard. We did the best we could with very basic living conditions.

Despite those basic and humble days I salute those fellow country people who, like me, travelled the distance in search of the truth, listened to the testimonies of the children, walked miles, shared rooms with strangers, climbed mountains and opened their hearts to the Gospa.

One season followed another and by the time I was on my third I was well and truly in love, not with a man but with the Mother of God, and a place where she chose to come to.

At the same time I'd had enough of the crowds, the heat, the non air-conditioned buses, the trekking up the mountains, and the complaints about the food, accommodation and more. I wanted to stay in Medjugorje but I didn't want the job. I wanted to part from the guide work and remember the good times, the great people I met, the leaders of groups who inspired me, the broken and wounded-hearted who were consoled, and the many Irish pilgrims who made it all worthwhile.

They say 'be careful what you pray for'; how right they are. At the end of my third season I fell in love and this time with a man. I didn't stand a chance. Medjugorje was now going to mean a lot more to me than a place where I had found God again, it would become the place where I was going to spend the rest of my life.

Walking down the aisle of St James Church while Fr Slavko Barbarić rendered 'Kraljica Mira' (Queen of Peace) I thought I was in a dream.

No sooner had I said the words 'I do' than war broke out and the dream became a nightmare. My new husband was no longer a financial accountant and budding entrepreneur but overnight was a conscripted soldier in a Croatian uniform, and sent to the front line for ten days at a time. I was about to enter my first class at the school of faith which lasts a lifetime. Fr Slavko Barbarić called on all foreigners to go home as war had swept from Croatia into Bosnia and Herzegovina. He looked me in the eye and told me, 'You are one of us now. You have to stay.'

Amidst calls from Ireland to come home, the horror that is war, the total evacuation of pilgrims, women and children, I settled into my new role as a wife to a local villager of Medjugorje, a shrine famous for the Apparitions of Our Lady. It proved a challenge not to be taken lightly.

Words like 'God give me the strength' or 'one day at a time, Sweet Jesus' come to mind as the best way to describe my first year of married life as I faced each day not knowing whether or not we would see one another ever again. But survive we did in spite of the chaos of war all around and with the help of the local priests and the visionaries we continued to honour the presence of Gospa in the same manner that has made the shrine the famous place of pilgrimage it is today. I felt and witnessed little fear but instead found myself surrounded by courage and great faith.

It was a dream to be able to understand and follow the messages given by Our Lady but when the dream became a nightmare I had to wake up and face the future, be that as it may.

In theory, how could one feel afraid for oneself and loved ones while sharing in the daily Apparitions of the Mother of us all? Unfortunately, the reality, even for the most faithful among us, can prove to be daunting at times. May I never forget the strength I received and the hope I felt as we gathered nightly in the cellar of the parish house with the visionaries, regardless of whether there were two or two hundred of us.

Well, thank God there was a future and, like everything else in life, the light appeared at the end of the tunnel, in this case war ended. We, unlike thousands of others, still had a home. Anything after this was sure to be a bonus.

Years later and the young generation rarely mention the war, the older generations have put the bitterness and disappointment in the past and have hope for the future and for the young democracy which is the state of Bosnia and Herzegovina.

It is obvious to the pilgrims today that the modern generation of villagers have been provided for far beyond all their expectations and dreams and that the poverty of their ancestors is firmly in the past. Living among them, I still see in them the villagers who despite great danger, human threats, and personal ridicule, answered the call of Gospa and opened their hearts and doors to us, and are still doing so today.

Twenty years later I'm still here, now well settled into village life and totally devoted to my family. When I was a guide I lived for Gospa and every word she said. Today I live *with* Gospa and sincerely hope she knows how grateful I am that she heard my prayers back then in 1989 at the foot of the cross on Apparition Hill.

Of course, many a prayer has been said since for myself, my family and my friends. And as is life, some have been answered and some have not, or were but in God's own way. One in particular brought me back to the same cross in 1994. After three years and one miscarriage I still hadn't been blessed with a child and was seriously aware of the great gift of life and was willing to do almost anything to get it. Kneeling before the cross, I promised to accept as many children as God would give me if I could hold my own child in my arms. Within the next ten years I had four boys and four girls.

Living with the supernatural events of Medjugorje on a daily basis is not an easy task and the ups and downs that mark our daily lives, along with the constant reminder of the messages Our Lady is asking us to adopt in our lives, can be at times too much for even the most committed among us.

But although we as human beings are 'faulty' from the day we are born and have earned our title as sinners, it doesn't mean that we can't change. I have found the message of Medjugorje, which is an echo of our gospel teaching, a major challenge and a challenge that will stay with me all my life.

Just because I live in the heart of the shrine it doesn't make the road to inner peace between myself and God any shorter for me than for those who from a distance have decided to turn their lives around. I find that it takes all my energy and peace of mind to raise my family of eight, who are now the present generation of the Ostojić family, in a manner that will reflect their rich history and their birthplace, the famous shrine of Medjugorje.

In the end, for those who believe, it is a lifetime commitment and a daily struggle, but I am sure that there are many who, like me, thank God for this small village between two hills.

What does Medjugorje mean to me?

It means the world, and it is my world. It doesn't mean that I am any better or closer to God but am a mere human being in God's plan for us, and living in Medjugorje doesn't exempt me from the trials of life. It doesn't mean that I don't get the crosses. I do and more but, God help us, I should know by now how to carry them.

19

Brian O'Driscoll

Brian O'Driscoll is a seminarian studying for the priesthood. It was the inter-cession of Our Lady of Medjugorje that saw him follow this path.
*   This is Brian's testimony.*

They say that if you want to make God laugh just tell him your plans. If this is truly the case, then God has been greatly entertained by my life before I really knew him, and by the plans and goals that I had created in my heart. For my plans led to a life of ruin, unhappiness and empti-ness. However, today my life is bursting with a wealth of treasure, but this treasure is not of the material sense of the word. This treasure is Jesus who dwells right at the centre of my heart. And I owe it all to the intercession of Our Lady of Medjugorje who never gave up on me, but embraced me with her motherly love and led me gently by the hand to her son Jesus. And she continues to do so every day.

In order to speak of my experience and encounters of Medjugorje, I must first travel back to my maiden voyage to that holy place five years ago when I was twenty-four years of age. What a journey it has been in such a short amount of time!

As I stood in the departure terminal of Cork airport on 8 September 2007 staring in the direction of the runway, I literally could not see past the windows as the fog that had descended on the area was so thick that all flights had to be delayed until it cleared just enough to allow the planes to take off.

My first thought was, 'Oh great! Why did I ever agree to come on this trip to the middle of nowhere in Bosnia and Herzegovina? This is the worst idea ever. I only did it to keep my mother happy and things have already started badly and can only get worse.' It was not that I had anything really against Medjugorje, because I had begun discovering my faith a few years earlier, but my idea of practising and developing my faith was to do it privately in my local church like I had done for the previous three years since Our Lady had brought me back to God through the rosary. However, work was piling up and this was probably the worst time to be heading away. And now this fog was delaying us even further. Eventually, after a five hour delay, the plane lifted off from Irish soil destined for the sunny shores of Dubrovnik in Croatia.

Three hours later we touched down on what I can only describe as one of the most beautiful locations that I have, personally, ever seen. We proceeded to collect our luggage and as we stepped out of the airport terminal to the warm autumn air, we were met by two beautiful young local women, Ozana and Marija, who would be our guides for the week. As the bus descended the hill towards the stunning and picturesque town of Dubrovnik, my heart began racing with excitement and anticipation but I did not know why. Little did I know that a life-changing experience lay ahead!

After a three-and-a-half hour bus journey, and what seemed like an eternity of rosaries, we finally arrived after nightfall outside St James Church in Medjugorje. As I stepped off of the bus, I distinctly remember looking around and thinking, 'What on earth have I done by coming here? I have to spend a whole seven days here! This will be a disaster!' When I look back at that moment now, I can always picture, in my mind, the image of Our Lady smiling down on me and comparing the vast difference between my plans for my own life and her son's plans for my life, and how the coming days would be the beginning of the most remarkable and amazing adventure that I could ever have had imagined.

Within three days I had visited Križevac, Apparition Hill, Fr Slavko's grave, and listened to the most remarkable of testimonies and talks. A fire had been re-ignited within me! I was on fire with the Holy Spirit and thirsting for God in a way that I have never experienced in my life. It was crazy, I could not explain it. I just knew that Our Lady was really present and that the purpose of my life was to love and serve God above all else. It was as if a blindfold had been lifted from my eyes and heart and I was truly seeing for the first time. I was head over heels in love with God and that burning love was growing and growing by the day. It was overwhelming yet so exciting at the same time. And for the first time in my life, I knew that God loved me and that if I was the only person that ever lived on this earth, he would still have died for me. In only three days, my life had been turned around through the graces and intercession of Our Lady of Medjugorje.

One of the nights as I knelt alone in front of the statue, I could feel the desire in my heart to give my entire life to serve God in some way.

However, I asked Our Lady to allow me to finish my work for the coming year, and then I would do whatever God wanted of me. The most remarkable of journeys was only beginning.

As the year progressed, my work got extremely busy, where I would be starting at 7.30 a.m. and finishing some nights at midnight. Slowly, my relationship with God began to slip away when I allowed my prayer to suffer due to the business of everyday life, and I found myself back in the same rut as I had originally been in. My work brought me to the UK, and then on to Australia. But I was very unhappy. I had money, cars, opportunities to see the world and be of the world, but the emptiness was growing within me once again. However, when Our Lady captures your heart once, she will never let it slip away again. In Australia I had a lot more free time on my hands and my prayer grew stronger and stronger. The deal that I had made with Our Lady kept entering my mind and grew stronger and stronger, until I knew that I could no longer continue to walk forward and ignore the voice of God through Our Lady. I prayed on it for a long time after and discerned that I was possibly being called to the priesthood, and I knew that I could no longer fight it.

This occurred in 2009, and once I returned from Australia, I applied to study for the priesthood with my diocese and was accepted very quickly afterward. Yet there was also a feeling deep within my heart telling me that I was not ready and if I was to enter the seminary, it would not be the right time now. However, I feared that this was my will telling me not to enter yet, and not the will of God. I longed to get to Medjugorje for a while to think this through, but I did not know how this would be possible. I prayed and prayed until one day a friend of mine put me in touch with an Irish priest who works with young people and helps them to discern what God has planned for their lives.

When I visited his house in Cork, he spoke with me and he told me to think about the things he had said to me and to return to him shortly with a decision whether or not to spend some time with him in the community. I thought about it, and decided that maybe this set-up did not suit me so I called the priest and left a voice message but never left my number. As far as I was concerned, that was that. However, Our Lady had other plans.

Three days later I was at a small parish event in Co. Kerry in the middle of nowhere. A friend had asked me to travel with him and I reluctantly agreed. It was a very enjoyable event, but to my dismay, as

I was walking out of the room at the break, there in front of me was the priest that I had spoken to a few days earlier. He ran straight up to me and said how he had been trying to contact me but could not get a number for me anywhere. Something had urged him to travel to Kerry also, and we both felt the hand of God in it. The priest told me how he has a house in Medjugorje where other young people stay also, and asked me to join him there. Two days later, we were on a flight bound for Medjugorje where I would spend almost three months. I arrived in Medjugorje in mid-May and was to stay until the middle of August. Our Lady was pulling all of the strings.

One night as I lay in my bed I could not sleep. It was 4 a.m. My heart was heavy and my mind was troubled. The curtains in my room were open, and from my bed I was staring straight across at the statue on Apparition Hill, which is always lit up at night time. I prayed from the depths of my heart for Our Lady to bring the peace of her son back to me, and for me to make the right decisions in my life. I felt that I was being called to the priesthood, yet I did not find peace with entering the seminary just now.

With that, something deep within me urged me to get up and climb Križevac. I was a little stunned because that mountain is never lit up at night and it would be very dark in the shadows of the trees and I would not be able to see where I was going over those dangerous rocks. Yet a burning desire within my heart urged me to get up and do it. I climbed out of my bed and it seemed as if my body was doing one thing by getting dressed, and my mind was telling me to do the opposite and get back into bed. However, I continued on.

I left the house and slipped into the dark of the night, moving underneath the shadow of that holy mountain. To this day I still cannot remember climbing that mountain, yet I know that I did because after leaving the house the next moment I could recall was standing in front of the huge white cross on top of Križevac. I slowly peered around me wondering how on earth I got here because I could not remember climbing the mountain.

My mind was so occupied with what lay ahead of me in life that I climbed the mountain without taking any notice of anything. Anyhow, I slowly ascended the steps to the cross, like a man about to buckle with the weight of the world on his shoulders. When I reached the summit, I slumped down on the wall around the base of the cross and began to pray a rosary very slowly. As I was halfway through the third decade, I stopped and gazed in awe at the sun that was just beginning to rise and spread its light throughout the beautiful countryside.

It was the most beautiful sight. Suddenly out of nowhere, I fell to my knees and began to cry, and I cried and cried for about fifteen minutes. I am not usually a crier and it stunned me because I did not know why I was crying. It just happened. Yet, looking back on it now, I can honestly say that it was the first time in my life where I completely surrendered to God.

My heart burst open to receive the graces that God wished for me to receive. And to this day I still vow that at that moment, it was as if I felt a pair of arms wrap themselves around me very gently. All of the burden and worry that I had experienced for so long was released through the tears. I jumped up and kissed the cross and finished my rosary with such joy, peace and happiness. With that I turned on my heels and skipped down the mountain. I felt so light and so at peace that I did not ever want to lose this feeling.

Two days later I was reading a book by the French nun, Sr Emmanuel, and in it was explained that Our Lady had once told one of the visionaries that every day as the sun rises in Medjugorje, she is always kneeling at the foot of the cross praying to her son. My heart nearly stopped at reading those words. I was instantly filled with happiness at the realisation that at the moment the sun was rising, I had felt two arms gently embrace me at the foot of the cross and this was the moment that Our Lady was praying to her son at the foot of the cross.

Today I am a seminarian studying for the priesthood. I do not know what God has in store for me in the future, but when I look back on my life I can see how God worked so many little miracles and blessings in my life. Back in 2009, God was calling me to priesthood but he was also telling me that the time was not right. Two years later, I entered and I thank God and Our Lady for that. Medjugorje was the turning point of my life with God. What Our Lady does for each of us is summed up in the second decade of the Mystery of Light where she tells us all to 'do whatever he tells you' as she points to her son Jesus. And that is what she has done for me. She has brought me closer to Jesus than I have ever been in my life. I do not know what the future holds, and I do not want to know. I trust in Jesus and entrust my entire life to him through his Holy Mother. That way, only the will of God will be done. In the words of Blessed John Paul II to Our Lady: '*Totus Tuus.*' (Totally Yours)

20

Daniel O'Donnell

Daniel O'Donnell is a world-renowned singer and songwriter. It was an unusual series of events that saw him travel over to Medjugorje and the inspiration he felt on the top of Apparition Hill one day led him to write the much adored hymn 'Sweet Queen of Peace of Medjugorje', which has raised a lot of money for charity.

This is Daniel's testimony.

I can't really remember the first time I heard about Medjugorje but there was an awareness there about the place which I most likely got through the media. However, I do remember thinking that I would like to go there some day and it was a funny series of events that finally saw me taking a trip over to the village for the first time.

A cousin of mine called Annette rang me late one night and told me that she had been praying and while she was doing so, she had this thought that I should go to Medjugorje. Although my cousin has a deep personal faith and she is a very good and kind person, she is not over the top when it comes to religion.

Immediately, I said to her, 'That's funny. I was actually thinking about going this summer.' So, in July 2002 I embarked on a journey over to the village of Medjugorje with a group from Waterford. There wasn't any particular reason why I was going there. I just felt the urge to visit the place. I already knew the priest who was with the group and a friend of mine also came with me for the trip.

We arrived in Medjugorje and we were staying in one of the locals' houses. The first morning, I got up and went down for breakfast and I was standing in the kitchen at the breakfast bar when I heard a woman's voice saying, 'Is that Daniel O'Donnell? That's not him! Is it him?'

The woman had a Donegal accent and so I turned around to her and said, 'It is me.'

The next thing she said to me was, 'Oh, we have been praying for you.'

I remember thinking to myself, 'Oh Lord, what is this all about?' I had just introduced Magella into the domain of my public life, and I thought the fact that she was divorced was the reason for them praying for me. So I was worried and thought to myself, 'Well here goes!'

However, the lady, called Briege, turned to me again and said, 'We have been praying for you since last September.' I knew then, instantly that this had nothing to do with my personal life as it was originating from months previous, when my relationship wasn't public knowledge and I thought to myself, 'Thank God for that.'

Briege's husband, Peter, turned around to her and said, 'Tell him what happened.' I was naturally curious and asked her what he was talking about but she said, 'Oh, I will tell you another time.'

We all got chatting and it turned out that they were from The Rosses in Donegal. Briege was born in Ranafast and Peter was born in Dungloe and I knew their families quite well. I was still very curious about what was said by Peter and eventually we sat down in a corner and she began to tell me her story.

She explained that she comes to Medjugorje quite regularly and while she was there the previous year, she got a message while in Mass one day.

For people who are not religious or know about Medjugorje, I suppose the 'message' is like a thought that you are sent, not necessarily a voice you actually hear.

However, the message she received was, 'Tell Daniel O'Donnell to go to Medjugorje.'

Briege was worried about how she could get the message to me and she told me that she came out of the chapel and didn't know how she could make this happen. She went back to Mass the following day and the same thing happened.

Both Briege and Peter were determined and they endeavoured to tell me this message that Briege had received. The third day she was at Mass and she came out thanking God that she hadn't heard a message today but Peter turned around and told her that he had received the message.

Earlier in 2002 there had been a function in our local hall as I was given a MBE and they both came down to the celebrations hoping to meet me. There were so many people there that Briege felt she couldn't tell me the message. She also called to the house I was living in and rang the doorbell but we were not in. Eventually, she asked a priest friend of hers, who I also knew, how would she go about getting this message to me?

The priest turned around to her and said that the best way to get the message to me was to tell my cousin Annette. They never actually verbally spoke to my cousin yet my cousin still rang me that night to say she had this thought, while praying, that I should go to Medjugorje.

After hearing this story on my first morning in the village, I knew it was going to be an eventful week, especially if it went on like this! I did all the normal things out there and found it to be the most peaceful place. I found the walk from St James Church to the Blue Cross at the bottom of Apparition Hill the most impressive thing for me out there. People who go to Medjugorje will know what I am talking about, but for those who don't; there is nothing religious about it but you walk through fields and vineyards and the tranquility and peacefulness is amazing. The sense of nostalgia I got when walking this path made me think of home when we were children. It brought back memories of lying down in the long, green grass on a hot summer's day and it was the most comfortable feeling for me.

On one of the days, we went up Apparition Hill. Briege and her husband Peter and their family had decided to climb the mountain and asked if I would like to join them. I said I would love to and we set off to climb the small mountain, Podbrdo.

We prayed on the way up and when we reached the top I sat down near to the Statue of Our Lady. All of a sudden, my head began to fill with words. The words came into my head:

> *I stood upon the hill above the village,*
> *And gazed down on the valley there below.*

I began to write the words down and within I few minutes, I had written a verse and a chorus to a hymn, which I called 'Sweet Queen of Peace'. It was not my intention to go out there to write a hymn but for whatever reason, I just did it.

Briege was sitting nearby and she came over to me and asked me what I was writing. I said to her, 'Do you know, I think I am writing a hymn about Medjugorje.'

Briege was thrilled on hearing this and I left it alone then and we set about descending the mountain. Later that week, we went up Cross Mountain, the bigger of the two, and I was sitting up at the top and once again I had this urge to write. It was here that I began to write the second verse.

Prior to that, a friend of mine called Josephine, had asked me was I going to use the word 'Medjugorje' in the song. I didn't think I would because I felt it was an awful hard word to fit into a song and I figured that people would know anyway what the song was about. I knew that if I was going to record it, I would have talked about it and its origins.

I wrote the last chorus:

Ave, Ave, Ave, Ave Maria,
We have come from lands both near and far.

The minute I wrote the word 'far' I thought to myself, 'Well that will rhyme with 'Medjugorje'.'

And so the last line of the song was:

Sweet Queen of Peace of Medjugorje.

This also became the title of the song.

I sang the song for Briege and she turned to me after I was finished and said, 'That is the reason you came here.'

That was the essence of my Medjugorje experience. I didn't see the sun spin or any rosary beads turning gold. There was nothing extraordinary, other than the peace, the tranquility and the writing of the hymn. I ended up writing a second hymn and we have raised a lot of money for various charities through the sale of both hymns.

When I was in Medjugorje, somebody asked me to sing the second hymn in a restaurant but I couldn't remember a word of it. So, I decided that I needed to go to the top of the mountain, where I was inspired to write it and sing it there. I wanted to go to the place where Our Lady appeared and sing it for the first time at that spot.

I headed off on my own one night with a hold-all on my back, a flash lamp in hand and my rosary beads with me. It was a beautiful, still night and the stars were clearly visible in the sky. I was at the foot of the hill, ready to negotiate the stones when I thought of the words:

Somehow when darkness falls, I feel you close to me.

I remember thinking to myself, 'Well I have my rosary beads in one hand and flash lamp in the other. How do you expect me to write like this?' It was an inopportune moment so I thought to myself that I would write it when I went home. I did just this and it became the second hymn called 'When Darkness Falls'.

My cousin Annette, who had phoned me that night and told me about her thought that I should go to Medjugorje, also told me her own story and experience of the place. Initially, she had no plans to go to Medjugorje but she received a call one night from a woman who told her that someone from her group had backed out and would she like to go on the pilgrimage in their place.

She told me that at that time, she had a question and she needed an answer to it. I don't know what the question was, as she didn't disclose that to me. After much thought, she decided to take the lady up on her offer and travelled out to Medjugorje.

One day, Annette was on her way to Mass but for some reason, she found herself turning towards the Blue Cross instead of towards the church. As she was walking, she found a pair of rosary beads on the ground. Tears came into her eyes and Annette began crying. Just recently, she had lost her mother and she said to Our Lady, 'I have no mother on earth anymore, you are my mother now. If the answer to my question is yes I want to find another pair of rosary beads and if I don't then I will know the answer is no.'

Annette knew it was quite presumptuous of her and quite demanding but she felt she needed to know.

It started to rain but she kept walking and when she got to the Blue Cross and was standing there praying, she heard a voice say, 'Hello.' As she was deep in prayer, she got a fright at first but it turned out to be a woman behind the bushes. The woman called her over and invited her to say the rosary together.

After some time of praying, an old man came along and Annette thought he looked a bit disheveled and that he may be a local.

The man walked up to the Blue Cross and began to desecrate the base of the cross by breaking things. All of a sudden he just picked something up and walked over to where both women were standing. He never looked at the other woman but took Annette's hands and put a pair of rosary beads into them. She asked him why he was doing this and he looked at her and said 'Sancta Maria' and then walked away. I still get shivers when I tell this amazing story.

What does Medjugorje mean to me?

I will always remember the great sense of peace out in Medjugorje. One day, I was walking down from Cross Mountain and I could hear the sound of singing travelling from the Dome at the back of the church right up to where I was. It was quite incredible.

I was present at one of Ivan's apparitions at the Blue Cross and also present for one of Marija's apparitions in the small church beside her house. At Marija's, I found it truly amazing the way she was praying and all of a sudden the praying stopped. Although I saw nothing, I knew Our Lady was there and present in a physical sense to her, but not to us. She was having a conversation but the rest of us couldn't hear her and then, all of a sudden, Marija came out of it and began praying again and it was like she was unaware of her surroundings.

My wife, Magella, went to Medjugorje on her own also and then we went back together for a second time. She found great solace and peace there during her visits. It is certainly a place I will visit again soon and I truly believe Our Lady is appearing over there.

I think a lot of people who go to Medjugorje seem to be seeking something, although they may not be too sure what it is. For me, I feel that there are more spiritual healings rather than physical healings and the peace you get while you are over there is immense. There is great power that can be really felt through prayer.

Writing the hymn was the furthest thing from my mind when I decided to go over there initially and yet the inspiration I felt on the small mountain that day became 'Sweet Queen of Peace of Medjugorje'.

21

James Mahon

James Mahon is the National Leader of Youth 2000 Ireland. While on his own spiritual journey, James visited Medjugorje and amidst many things found great renewal in the sacrament of Reconciliation. He also tells of the strong connection the Youth 2000 movement has with Medjugorje.

This is James' testimony.

My first encounter with Medjugorje was in 2004. I was then a 23-year-old student who was taking my first baby steps on a road to conversion. I found myself in Emmanuel House, Clonfert, Co. Galway, in a house of prayer run by Eddie and Lucy Stones. I had never heard anyone proclaim the truth of our faith like Eddie before. I didn't know anything about my faith but I knew what he was saying was true because my heart was on fire.

A chap called Seán was promoting a book on Medjugorje and I felt compelled to buy one. I devoured the book that same evening. I could not believe that I had not heard about this before: the apparitions, the visionaries, Our Lady's messages, the places and the people. The author really made Medjugorje come alive for me. I could nearly picture myself on the hills, the mountains and in St James Church.

I made a firm commitment in my heart to go there. I didn't know how but I guessed if it was meant to be, somehow it would happen. I discovered that Eddie Stones himself was bringing a group in June that year and I vowed to scrape the money together somehow. It all managed to come together without much hardship and soon enough I found myself in Dubrovnik airport feeling a bit of trepidation, wondering what the hell I was letting myself in for.

The three-hour bus journey to Medjugorje was painful enough to be honest, as was the enthusiasm of everyone on the bus who had been there before. It took me a day or two to get into the whole thing, especially the heat because, being a typical freckled Irish person, I burn to a crisp in the sun! I could, however, feel a real profound peace around the place from the moment I arrived – it was uncanny, something I had never experienced before. I really wondered what the week had in store for me.

They say when you go to Medjugorje that you enter into the 'School of Mary' and that she gently, as any mother would, shows you the ways of her son Jesus. That was true for me. I was starting to find this inner peace which I had never experienced before, and the more the week went on, the more I fell in love with the place and the more authentic I believed the apparitions were.

All the many rosaries I prayed during that week convinced me that this faith lark was for real and to keep on the road of conversion. I think if I had not gone to Medjugorje at that early stage of my conversion, I probably would not have kept going with the whole faith thing. In that first pilgrimage, Mary guided me by the hand (through her rosary) and introduced me to her son Jesus. Where did I encounter this same Jesus you might ask? I will tell you where, through the sacrament of Confession.

Medjugorje is often called the confessional of the world because many people, like me, experience this sacrament anew. I had never truly understood the need or value of it. When on that first pilgrimage I made that first honest, proper confession of my life, I felt that I had truly experienced the love of Christ for me for the first time in my life. By way of explanation, the priest by his ordination receives the Holy Spirit, the spirit of Christ to forgive sins, so he therefore forgives our sins in the person of and with the authority of Christ.

After that confession I could somehow feel that a weight was lifted from my shoulders. I felt a certain inner freeness that I had never experienced before and I also felt as if the healing hand of Christ had touched me in the place where those sins and sufferings had pained me. You can tell people until you are blue in the face about the love that Christ has for them, but until they experience this real, tangible love for themselves, they will never believe you. That's the way it was with me too.

When I got home from that pilgrimage I vowed to continue to say my prayers and to hang in there with God in order to embark on the plan that he had for my life, whatever that may be. They say that when you come home that's when the pilgrimage really starts. It sounds like a cliché but it's very true. In Christmas 2005, I went to my first Youth 2000 retreat. As it happened, some lady in Medjugorje had told me about Youth 2000 but it had taken me a bit of time to finally get to one of their events.

The young people I met at that first Youth 2000 retreat reminded me of the young people that I had met in Medjugorje. The spirituality of the retreats was also very similar. By way of explanation, Youth 2000 is a spiritual movement established to draw young people, through Mary, to a deep and lasting union with the Eucharistic Heart of Jesus Christ. In a nutshell, we in Youth 2000 aspire to show other young people the treasure their Catholic faith is, and to show them that they can have a personal relationship with Jesus Christ by the quickest and safest means, through the intercession of his mother Mary, the one who knew him best.

Our motto is 'Youth leading youth to the heart of the Church'. We carry out our mission in Ireland by organising twenty weekend retreats annually for young people between the ages of sixteen and thirty-five. We also have thirty-five youth prayer groups around the country too. Youth 2000 was a means of keeping the genuine personal encounter with Christ experienced in Medjugorje alive.

The spirituality of Youth 2000, the biggest Catholic youth movement in Ireland, and Medjugorje bear many similarities. The obvious ones being the key and central role of Jesus truly present in the Eucharist and also the key role of Mary. As a means of describing where Youth 2000 originated from, I will give you some background information. In 1989 Pope John Paul II welcomed the youth of the world to Santiago de Compostela in Spain for the fourth World Youth Day. As the last decade of the twentieth century was dawning, the Holy Father invited them to take an active part in the Decade of Evangelisation leading up to the Great Jubilee Year 2000.

He called on the young people especially to 'become shining heralds of the re-evangelisation and generous architects of a new civilisation of love and truth'. Among the thousands of young people present at Santiago de Compostela in 1989, Ernest Williams, a young English man then aged twenty-six, listened attentively to the words of the Holy Father. Ernest understood that the call of the Holy Father inviting the young people themselves to be the first witnesses of Jesus in the Third Millennium was essential. Immediately after World Youth Day he made a pilgrimage to Fatima. It was during a period of prayer and reflection in the presence of the blessed sacrament that an image came to him of a chain of young people in adoration around the world by the end of the Decade of Evangelisation. This was to be the vision of a new spiritual initiative within the Church called Youth 2000, an initiative that through Eucharistic Adoration would draw young people back to the truth, lead-ing them away from a life without hope. Through a rediscovery of the

Sacrifice of the Holy Mass, adoration of the blessed sacrament, the Holy Scriptures, the sacrament of Reconciliation, and devotion to Mary, young people would discover in prayer the unique calling that they had to live as Christians.

The first Youth 2000 Festival of Prayer or Retreat was launched in Medjugorje in 1990. For one week, 7,000 young people gathered from twenty-four countries of the world to celebrate Mass, to listen to the Word of God, to receive his forgiveness in the sacrament of Reconciliation, to pray together and to listen to teaching sessions given by the many priests present. Throughout the entire festival there was adoration of the blessed sacrament, giving them an opportunity to come and spend time with Jesus.

Instrumental to this festival taking place were Ernest Williams, Fr Slavko Barbaric and Fr Liam Lawton. In the short period after that first Youth 2000 festival in Medjugorje, Youth 2000, as it is known today, officially started in England, Ireland, USA, Germany. That festival also gave birth to the Medjugorje International Youth festival, which is now entering into its twenty-third year and now attracts up to 40,000 young people annually.

So, Youth 2000, the young Catholic organisation that gives hope to so many young people in Ireland, is forever indebted to Medjugorje for that first festival. In some small way, I would also like to think that the Medjugorje International Youth festival is somewhat indebted to Youth 2000 for showing them the ropes!

Youth 2000 has no official connection to Medjugorje and we, like everyone else, await the definitive ruling of the Church with respect to the apparitions and the visionaries. Irrespective of the authenticity of the apparitions and the visionaries, I believe that what you experience in Medjugorje is an experience of a proper Christian community similar to the early Christian community as described in chapter two of the Acts of the Apostles.

I was struck from my first pilgrimage at how united all the people were. Regardless of whether they were from Killybegs, Kilkenny or Kentucky, there was absolutely no pretence or agenda in any of the many chats I had with other pilgrims. It is like we are all in this together, all God's family. This real genuine Christian love that I encounter in Medjugorje strikes me very deeply every time I go back. This proper Christian community feeling continues in the Masses, prayer and adoration of the blessed sacrament. The faith of the people around you makes these times of worship even more powerful. It's not like at home where people leg it out of Mass after Holy Communion. In Medjugorje people always manage to give it their best, the way it really should be.

I am convinced that Medjugorje has indirectly renewed that Catholic faith in this country and in many places around the world. The many thousands of Irish people who have gone over the years have surely made a real impact back home. The main thing Medjugorje has done is that it has shown the ordinary layman that he can have a personal relationship with Jesus and his mother Mary. This is not something wacky, this is something real, something life-changing. Eucharistic Adoration is crucial to the renewal of the Church in Ireland and I believe that many people who are involved in initiatives that promote Eucharistic Adoration, came to a knowledge of Jesus' true presence in Medjugorje.

Medjugorje is also the place that the most hardened sinner can go and get consolation. So often I have had parents come to me about their children, and also children come to me about their parents. They usually say they would love if their loved one came to know their faith. If it is a particularly difficult case I always say, 'Send them to Medjugorje, get them on the plane and Our Lady will meet them where they are at.' It has a one hundred per cent success rate in my eyes. Every hard case, cynic, atheist, agnostic or addict I know who has gone to Medjugorje has got something out of it, has found their faith on some level, has come back changed and wants to go back again. My motto is 'Get them on a plane, Mary will do the rest'.

I have met others in church circles who would be harsher critics of Medjugorje than most atheists. These, in my eyes, normally fall into two categories. Firstly, there are those who would be petrified of going because they believe that if they do go, they might be called to a greater level of holiness than they are already exhibiting in their lives. They normally justify the question of Medjugorje by saying it's a counterfeit, that they are the only ones who have figured out this big so-called conspiracy, whereas they believe all the millions of people who have gone over the years are a crowd of eejits!

If these people somehow manage to go, they are normally melted by the whole Medjugorje experience and then become its biggest promoters. Secondly, there are the ones who deem themselves too highbrow or intellectual to believe in what they call nonsense. There is normally an element of what you might call 'spiritual snobbery' here, and these people, if they take a punt and go, normally have a proper conversion of heart which maybe they did not have before.

As for me I would gladly go back to Medjugorje in a heartbeat. I try to go once a year now and I feel like I experience a slice of heaven every time I go back. People sometimes find it strange that I want to go back again and again. It is hard to explain to them why, but they always know when they go themselves. There is such a profound peace there and why would you not go and recharge your batteries? It's such an oasis of peace and I believe that this is down to the Queen of Peace.

22

Anne Corcoran

Anne Corcoran is proprietor of The Westport Plaza Hotel and The Castlecourt Hotel in Co. Mayo. A seed of love for Medjugorje was planted in her heart after her first trip in 1987. Friends of Anne have also found solace in the village during difficult times in their lives.

This is Anne's testimony.

My first of many trips to Medjugorje dates back to 1987. A friend of mine called Terry invited me on this trip with her brother-in-law Francis. To be honest I hadn't even heard of the place and hadn't a clue where it was but, as they were kind enough to offer me a ticket, I decided to go along.

It was a trip that in many ways changed my life. Twenty-six years later I find myself being 'drawn back' to it time and time again to meet what were once strangers but who have now become close friends. It's hard to define what it is that attracts me to Medjugorje but it has become a place that is very personal to me.

On that first trip all three of us headed off with different expectations and a great week was had by all. Francis entertained us along the way with his beautiful singing. Terry – who has a strong faith – seemed to absorb everything that was going on in Medjugorje at that time. On the other hand, I had gone there with no real expectations and most of the time felt like an observer looking in from the outside.

We shared a small room in a very modest family home. Street lighting along the paths to Podbrdo, the Blue Cross and Cross Mountain (Križevac) was limited and so it was necessary for us to carry flashlights when we were out after dark. We climbed the hills and along the paths we met many locals. I sampled the local schnapps that was brewed in large pots over open fires. The schnapps tasted strong and I remember thinking it tasted like Poteen (an Irish equivalent), not as strong though and a little sweeter. It certainly put a pep in my step – a taste of a different kind of spirit!

During the trip we travelled to Dubrovnik on a day excursion. While Francis searched for a phone to ring his beloved wife back in Ireland,

Terry and I prayed the rosary with the beads in our hands walking along the beach and laughing at the thought of what the folks back home would say if they could see us now.

I realise I was not spiritually uplifted during my first trip. Nevertheless, a very small seed of love for Medjugorje was sowed in my heart that has continued to blossom to this day. I came home with beautiful memories and a strong sense and understanding of people's love for Our Lady. It was a real eye-opener witnessing it at first hand.

I remembered fondly a very big church in a very small village and a large gathering of locals in front of St James Church, stretching to where Our Lady's statue stands today.

I was moved by the young people in particular on their knees praying the evening prayers and it seemed this was their normal day's practice. Their devoutness astounded me. I also remember many women praying in the fields. When we walked passed them they would call 'Gospa' in reverence and with clasped hands they looked up to heaven as if they were saying, 'Our Lady is here.'

In 2000 I revisited Medjugorje and the small seed sown thirteen years previously seemed eager to grow. It felt as though I was going home and my faith deepened. I witnessed many miraculous healings and started to articulate to others the wonderful devotion to Our Lady that existed there. This in turn encouraged many of my friends to visit Medjugorje.

As I became more spiritually invigorated, my trips became much more regular and for many years now I have made a number of visits to the Shrine annually. One of the special healings that I witnessed was that of a young man called Keith. He was in many ways a typical seventeen-year-old who enjoyed life but had sadly begun taking drugs as well as drinking far too much for his own good.

His behaviour had resulted in a couple of court appearances and he was due to serve a short jail sentence on his return from his trip to Medjugorje. Why Keith ever agreed to go to Medjugorje was a mystery to me but he experienced a life-changing conversion during his pilgrimage. On his return, Keith duly showed up in court and he explained to the judge that he intended to mend his ways. He appeared genuine and to the amazement of all present, the judge decided to give him a second chance. Keith embraced the opportunity with determination and sincerity. He gave up drugs and alcohol and spent a lot of time in adoration.

Two years later he initiated a series of trips that saw him bring groups of teenagers on pilgrimage to Medjugorje.

Keith is now a fine young 25-year-old who has unreservedly dedicated his life to Jesus and Mary. He is currently training to be a priest with the Order of the Alliance of the Two Hearts in the Philippines.

Recently, Keith made a short trip home and it was a delight to personally witness his transition. The once turbulent, frustrated and lost teenager was transformed into a 25-year-old man of compassion whose faith and love for Our Lady and Jesus had truly made him a man of God.

There are many other vivid examples of how Medjugorje has changed the lives of those who choose to go there. In 2009, I climbed Cross Mountain (Križevac) with a few friends – amongst them were Liam and Anne, who had tragically lost their youngest son Daniel earlier that year. Naturally they were devastated and broken.

The tragedy was still raw and they had come to Medjugorje for no reason in particular – it just seemed the right thing to do at the time. I remember praying that something would happen on their pilgrimage that would give them comfort.

As we ascended the holy mountain we noticed a young boy – no more than twelve years of age – lagging closely behind us with his parents and what appeared to be a stray dog. We reached the top and finished our stations of the cross. Liam decided to get a few photos and the young boy eagerly volunteered to take the pictures and he assured Liam he knew how to use the digital camera.

The photos were duly taken and as the young boy handed back the camera, Anne casually asked him his name. He replied 'Daniel'. Silence ensued and for those of us fortunate to be there on that morning we realised that someone or something somewhere was 'at work'. Tears filled Anne and Liam's eyes and the sense of emotional healing was almost palpable. When I tell this story to others they suggest that it may have just been a coincidence. Perhaps it was – or was it?

I certainly can't explain the many other coincidences that are regularly happening in Medjugorje. Perhaps we should refer to them as 'God incidences'? What happened on the mountain that morning was a small consolation to Anne and Liam and a sign that Jesus in his compassion knew their suffering and the huge void they had in their heart at the loss of their dearest son Daniel. To this day Liam and Anne talk about that morning and if nothing else it has given them the will to carry on and accept the cross they have been asked to carry.

St Thérèse of the Little Flower said that she would send roses as a sign that she is interceding for people in need and many people have experienced this. In a similar way, I believe that the little boy called Daniel, who accompanied us, was a little sign from God. As we know he works in mysterious ways.

Last Easter I was delighted to make yet another trip to what my friend Jim Browne would lightly call 'the live show', as Our Lady is still appearing there after thirty-two years. Easter is always a nice time of the year. We usually arrive just in time for Easter Sunday, which is a special time as Jesus our Saviour has just been raised from the dead.

At one of the Masses in St James Church that week an Irish priest gave a lovely homily and asked what the purpose of a pilgrimage was? Someone who goes on a pilgrimage 'prays with his feet and experiences with all of his senses that his entire life is one long journey to God'. I can only aspire to that thought and so I keep going back to Medjugorje to be reminded of my purpose in life.

There are many aspects of Medjugorje that appeal to me. We usually travel with Marian Pilgrimages under the guidance of David Parkes and the guides Danijela, Thea, Mojca and Ozana. David himself had an amazing personal healing experience that he is always willing to share with anyone he meets. He is a true witness to Medjugorje. It is obvious from the way the guides speak that they continue to be uplifted even through their working days in Medjugorje.

One of the guides told me she still continues to be inspired when Vicka, one of the visionaries, gives her talk. But, then again, all the visionaries are so inspiring. I think particularly of Vicka – that smile of love on her radiant face as she ignites when she speaks about the love that Our Lady has for each one of us.

There are many things one can do as a pilgrim in Medjugorje and over the years you tend to gravitate more to certain things and you plan your own little routine that you look forward to. For me, I enjoy getting up at 5.45 a.m. and sampling the peace and quiet as I walk to Križevac mountain. I then climb the mountain to do the way of the cross, the *Via della Rosa*. It's a very special place that genuinely makes me feel the suffering that Jesus endured for each one of us and it also makes me think of his Blessed Mother and the pain that she carried in silence knowing that it was his chosen path.

'God pursues us in our restlessness, receives us in our sinfulness, holds us in our brokenness.' I really like that quote from Scotty Smith. I have witnessed God working in the brokenness of our lives. My own sister Mary sadly lost her husband David some years ago. He was just fifty-one years old and left behind a devoted wife and eight beautiful children. The many graces and consolations Mary receives can be attributed to her great trust in Jesus, in spite of her huge loss. She has been given great strength to embrace her cross. Mary has visited Medjugorje on numerous occasions with her younger children and this has helped her immensely as she tries to pass on her faith to her children.

Adoration in Medjugorje is a unique and special experience. Jesus is exposed in a magnificent monstrance. This, coupled with beautiful and uplifting music and hymns sung in different languages, creates an atmosphere of oneness with Christ. Every time I attend adoration, I know I am in the true presence of Jesus and that he showers me with his love and graces. In adoration I trust that Jesus is looking after me and all whom I bring before him in prayer.

In adoration, I feel Jesus fills me with his love and kindness in order for me to bring it to others. When I come home I hope I bring some of that love, peace and kindness with me. I often wish I could bring more. Our Lady said in an earlier message on 25 February 1995: 'I invite you to become missionaries of my message … I invite you to live with love the messages I give, and to transmit them to the whole world, so that a river of love flows to people who are full of hatred and without peace.'

What has Medjugorje done for me and how has it changed my life? This is a very complex question to be able to give a simple answer. Firstly, my many visits to Medjugorje have made me realise that all graces come from Jesus and Our Lady who is our blessed Mother. She is guiding us along the path of holiness.

Secondly, I love the little trickles of peace that slowly emerge when I spend time in reflection and prayer in Medjugorje. It never comes in gushing waves or loud bolts of thunder – just regular trickles that ease my thirst just enough to help me to understand the important things in life and more importantly its true meaning. I find praying a challenge but I find praying in Medjugorje a lot easier.

Above all, Medjugorje has helped me deal, in a Christian way, with the numerous people I deal with on a daily basis as part of our hotel business in Westport. For that I must credit my amazing mother May whose strong faith has been a powerful influence on the entire family.

From very humble beginnings, her influence and encouragement were instrumental in developing our business to what it is today. We are so blessed that at eighty-six years of age she can still travel with us to Medjugorje. That is something I thank God and Our Lady for every day. My dad – a kind, unassuming and gentle soul – sadly passed away in 2003 and I miss him dearly. I hope his kind nature has seen him through the heavenly gates.

In the lobby of our hotel I recently hung a painting of Our Lady embracing Pope John Paul II. I bought the painting many years ago in Medjugorje but only recently found the perfect spot for it. It now has found its rightful home and it is my way of expressing my gratitude for the love Our Blessed Mother has for all of us.

Thankfully the hotel can be used from time to time for prayer meetings and for gatherings of small religious groups. One of the first such meetings was held here in 2001 for a talk about Medjugorje and the opportunity was used to encourage people to take a pilgrimage there. Every year we have a Medjugorje pilgrims reunion led by Jim Browne who brings groups to Medjugorje twice a year.

The last meeting was one of the most successful with more than 500 people in attendance. The meeting started with the Divine Mercy devotion, a personal testimony and finished with Mass celebrated by Fr Benny McHale. We also had songs of praise from David Parkes, the Vard Sisters, James Kilbane and Annette Griffin. Days like these are precious as it's lovely to take time out of this busy world we live in to give thanks and praise to God.

Hotel life is busy, but for the most part it is very enjoyable and equally challenging. However, it can also have many distractions, not only from a business point of view but also from a social aspect. I go through stages when I struggle with prayer and feel God is far away from me or, more to the point, I am far away from him. I am still learning that faith is not a feeling but more of a trust in God.

Nevertheless, I try to put a little order into my life. The time spent in Medjugorje has certainly helped me achieve this and it has also helped me to shape my faith. In the mornings I try to spend some time in quiet prayer as I reflect on the readings and gospel for the early morning Mass. I use some reflections that help to make the Mass more meaningful and relevant to everyday life. I now realise that no day is wasted when I attend Mass as it deepens my faith and brings me closer to God.

I live in the beautiful town of Westport, which nestles in the shadow of Croagh Patrick, known locally as The Reek. We are surrounded by indescribable beauty and infinite nature and it is only appropriate that we thank our Creator for the things around us that we too often take for granted. Every morning, I go for a walk after Mass on a small country road with my two sisters, Ger and Mary. We pray the rosary and of course have our little girly chats too.

On the way back we see our own holy mountain in the distance. It's not Križevac or Podbrdo but it has many of the same messages to impart to those who wish to listen. My other walking friends – namely Sheila and my sister-in-law Anne Marie – have now affectionately named our daily routine as our 'Medjugorje Walk'. Some mornings we are also joined by my school friend Mary O'Brien who is a great believer in the fruits of Medjugorje. She got engaged to be married to her soulmate Frank at the Blue Cross in Medjugorje in 2005.

I am very grateful to Mary for introducing me to a very special person, Aine Simovic, who was married to Tony and lived with their four children in Čitluk just outside Medjugorje. We became very close in the latter days of her life. Although I only knew Aine for a short period she was a real inspiration to me. She battled with cancer in a courageous and brave manner. We had so much in common and shared the same sense of humour. Aine once talked about the love of God and embracing one's cross, which she certainly did in a very dignified way. Sometimes God puts people into our lives for a time to help one another along life's pilgrim journey. I believe Aine was one of these special people and she is sadly missed but not forgotten. May she rest in peace.

As I mentioned earlier, I went on my first trip without any understanding of what was really happening there. In 1981 Our Lady said, 'I am choosing this parish in a special way and I want to guide it.' She further emphasised this on 25 March 1985 when she said, 'I am choosing this parish in a special way, which is dearer to me than others, where I joyfully went when the Almighty sent me.'

Personally, if I had any doubt that Our Beloved Lady was appearing in Medjugorje those words convince me with a vigour and conviction like no other that there is a daily presence there. It is only in more recent years that I am beginning to appreciate what her messages are saying to us and their relevance to the world we live in today.

Fr Slavko once said, 'The more we meet those messages and are living with them, the more we talk about them, the more we think about them, the more we see that every single message, even if it is very simple, is important.'

Finally, I would like to conclude by saying that Medjugorje means different things to different people. For me it means a lifelong journey of faith, something that I started many years ago with no 'terms and conditions' – just an open heart. It's a journey where you will find a special happiness and a journey that I would encourage anyone who is reading this to embark on with an open heart.

23

Jackie 'The Farmer' O'Sullivan

Jackie O'Sullivan is from Killarney, Co. Kerry. On Holy Thursday 2012, he celebrated his 100th birthday. He has been to Medjugorje many times and in 2012 climbed to the top of Križevac.
This is Jackie's testimony.

My name is Jackie O'Sullivan but people know me better as Jackie 'The Farmer'. I was born on 5 April 1912 and so on Holy Thursday 2012 I celebrated my 100th birthday.

Growing up in Ireland and being Catholic, religion was very important to my family and me. It was different from today; the prayers had not yet been shortened and it was important for us to say the rosary every day.

Some years back, I heard people talking about Medjugorje and I was very interested. I had been to Lourdes and The Holy Land on pilgrimage but I felt anxious to go to Medjugorje.

I went to Medjugorje for the first time in 2001 with Bridie McCarthy's group and have travelled with Bridie's group each time since then.

I fell in love with the village very much and adored everything about it including the people and how they practise their religion. I have travelled halfway around the world to places including The Holy Land and Lourdes but I love Medjugorje the most.

I have been on pilgrimage many times to the village and on my last trip I climbed to the top of Križevac. The vineyards are so beautiful and I love the way you pass through the fields to get to the mountains. One of the things I liked about staying in the people's houses was the way you had your own key to get into the house when you wished. We were very welcome to the freedom of the kitchen where all facilities were available to us and this made us feel at home instantly. This made things very easy and things are very well carved out over there.

While in Medjugorje, I also visited the Mother's Village and we had a beautiful Mass out there, which was a lovely experience. I went everywhere and did everything I possibly could.

On my last visit in May 2012 I climbed Apparition Hill on the Monday. The following day, I decided to climb Križevac, the bigger of the two mountains. The rain was pouring down and when we reached the third station, we had to wait a while as the rain was so heavy. I was determined to go on and after about twenty minutes the rain cleared and so I climbed to the top along with my good friends, Denis Dineen and Tom Mullins.

It was breathtaking to stand at the top of the mountain and look at the whole countryside. Denis approached a young guy from Argentina and said to him, 'Could I ask you a favour? I have a man with me who has turned 100 years this year and I don't have a camera at the moment, could you take a photograph with yours and send it on to me?' The young guy was overwhelmed and got so excited as he said he had never seen a person who was 100 years old! He duly forwarded the photographs by email.

Climbing Križevac knocked a good bit out of me but it was something that I wanted to do and it felt really good to get to the top.

Also on this trip, I had not one but three celebrations for my birthday including one in Marina's home where we stayed. The second one was in Victor's restaurant and the third in Colombo's, which went on until one in the morning with plenty of traditional Irish singing led by Tom Mullins, followed by Bridget Nolan, Ellen Moylan and others.

The first year we became very friendly with the owners of Kathy's Kitchen, a Dublin girl and her Croatian husband. In the early years it was the only place to get an Irish breakfast. We have called to them every year since then. This year she gave me a beautiful statue of the Sacred Heart as a present for my 100th birthday. Also for my 100th birthday I got a set of rosary beads specially made in Medjugorje from Bridie McCarthy; it was decorated with one letter on each bead spelling 'Congratulations, Jackie, on your 100th birthday'.

Also, if we feel homesick while in Medjugorje, we can go to Victor's restaurant where he serves Irish breakfasts.

The reason I go back to Medjugorje all the time is because I love the people, I love the lectures. I love going to Fr Slavko's grave in the graveyard, the mysteries of light, the statue of the risen Christ, and the low Stations of the Cross. I love the mountains, the fields and the lovely weather. It is so lovely to see the blossoms in the fields and the women selling the handwoven tablecloths on the way up to the mountain. I bought some of these tablecloths as gifts each year, one of which is laid out on my table at home. Also to see so many priests on the altar at Mass is amazing especially as it is such a beautiful church.

We hired a car one day and went to Mostar. The taxi driver got us a tour of Mostar Catholic Cathedral even though the Cathedral was locked to the public. We also saw the bishop's palace and went to see where the river Neretva rises under the dry mountain; an amazing sight.

We saw where the remains of the old Mostar Bridge, which was destroyed during the war, are. The bridge was rebuilt by the United Nations troops, of which some members were Irish.

We went by coach to Lubuski to visit St Joseph the Worker's home, built for the old and destitute left homeless after the war. The home was set up by two American ladies, Sr Muriel and Mary Walsh. Large contributions from Ireland and elsewhere helped to establish this home. The chapel in this home is known as the Irish chapel and one of our Kerry priests, Fr Donal O'Connor, brought from Ireland a large Celtic cross in remembrance of a young man who died tragically. This Celtic cross now is permanently in the Irish Church. The pilgrims, residents and staff attended Mass celebrated by Fr Brendan Walsh this year.

We enjoyed tea and biscuits after the Mass and entertained the residents with a sing-song and also a little dance. Surrounding St Joseph's home there are trees planted with plaques on them in remembrance of some of the past pilgrims and their families that have passed on to their eternal reward.

On our return journey we stopped off in Humac to visit St Anthony's Church and each of the pilgrims was blessed with the relic of St Anthony by Fr Brendan Walsh. We made one more stop at the waterfall, which was beautiful but nothing compared to our Torc waterfall in Killarney.

In my first years visiting Medjugorje, I went to Cenacolo, where Mirjana used to have her apparitions on the second of each month. Large numbers used to attend including many Italians. The stillness and silence at the moment of the apparition was evident, something supernatural was taking place. It gives me great hope when I go to Cenacolo and listen to the young men giving their testimonies and to see how they have recovered from their addictions, the progress they have made through following the programme introduced by Sr Elvira and how God has worked in their lives.

We also travel to Surmanci by coach, a very winding and steep road, for Mass. There is a special icon in that church.

In the earlier years, we used to go to the church of the Oasis of Peace and spend some time in adoration of the blessed sacrament. The crucifix in that church left a lasting memory and impression on me.

For the first five years that I went to Medjugorje, we used to always go to Siroki Brijeg to listen to Fr Jozo's lectures and to pray with him. It didn't matter how many times I heard Fr Jozo speak, it was always as impressive and informative as the first time I heard him. He told us of the story of the thirty Franciscan martyrs slain by communists on 5 February 1945. We saw the tomb where the thirty martyrs were buried.

On each pilgrimage I made many new and true friends. One such friend was the late Pádraig Ó Dálaigh, a native Irish speaker from Waterville, Co. Kerry, who went to Medjugorje for the first time in the year 2000 at the age of eighty-one. We went on seven pilgrimages together. I looked forward to meeting him each year. We talked and reminisced about our younger days. He passed to his eternal reward in February 2012.

Today Medjugorje is known as the confessional of the world. Lines of those waiting for confession are extremely long. Thirty to forty priests sit and hear confessions in many different languages for five to six hours, sometimes well after 10 p.m. The statue of St Leopole (the patron of a good confession) is situated close to the confessionals at the left-hand side of the church, which were completed in the year 2001. Extra confessionals were required. These were constructed in late 2011 and finished in 2012 and are situated on the right-hand side of the church.

On one of my visits to Medjugorje, I bought two pairs of large rosary beads which I brought home with me and placed on two graves – my parent's grave and my wife's grave. My wife Rita passed away thirty-nine years ago this Christmas. I also lost a child called Hannah Mary who died at only three weeks old. In Medjugorje, I feel close to my wife and all the memories come back to me.

Buíochas le Dia don saol fada atá faighte ag Seán.

24

Margaret Toomey

Margaret Toomey is an actress who is well known for playing the part of Eileen Bishop in the long running popular Irish soap Fair City. *Margaret has been to Medjugorje twice.*

This is Margaret's testimony.

When I was asked to write my testimony my first reaction was panic. I thought: 'I don't do this sort of thing and anyway I have no gift for writing.' I was in Medjugorje for the second time and still struggling to articulate the experience for myself. How could I do it for anyone else? I really was struggling. There was no doubt but this was a very prayerful place. The devotion of the pilgrims was humbling and I found a renewed belief in the power of prayer.

The special peace that everyone seemed to experience here was still a mystery. Was it the same peace I felt at the top of a mountain in West Cork as I gazed down on the wonders of God's Creation? Do you have to go to a specific physical place to get the grace to experience this peace? Was the peace and blessing of Medjugorje available to those who had no way of making a trip to this holy place? I just couldn't truthfully tell you that I was immediately overwhelmed by the place in some spectacular spiritual way. The only way I can think of telling you about the experience is to start with a story – a kind of a parable.

The Little Girl and the Musician

The little girl stood at the gate waiting for the musician to pass. She couldn't remember a time when he wasn't part of her life. He would pass by the gate every day as she played in the garden. He would always stop and talk to her. His face was kind and they laughed a lot. As she grew older they became great friends. They talked about many things. He laughed with her when she was happy and comforted her when she was sad, and when life was difficult he stayed close by and sent his many friends to support her.

She discovered that he was the conductor of a great orchestra. He taught her to play music and eventually she learnt to play a few chords on the guitar. There was a time when she would never miss a performance of his but then her life became busy and her commitments numer-

151

ous. She saw him most days as he passed her house and they would always exchange a few words or maybe take the time to share a coffee. Although she always tried to be present at his big concerts, they rarely found time these days to play music together. However, he was still her good friend and their encounters continued.

One day she received an invitation from him to play the guitar in his orchestra at a big international gathering. She protested that she was rusty and hadn't played for years but he assured her that he had a place for her in his orchestra and needed her to complete the sound he wanted.

The journey was long and exciting. She was enthralled by the strange and beautiful sights she passed along the way. She was apprehensive but looking forward to what he promised would be a unique experience. It was evening when she arrived at the hall. Hundreds of musicians were already in place. They were tuning their instruments. They all seemed to know the music and were playing in wonderful harmony. There seemed no place for her few miserable guitar chords. She went inside and felt very alone. She tried to discover what music they were playing but the answer was always the same. She just had to be here and the music would come to her. She sat at the back and played tentatively. She knew she played badly. She should have been better prepared before she came. There was a lot to learn. In that moment she realised that her work would only begin when she got home.

In Medjugorje I was that girl. I had always been aware of the power of God's presence in my life and was grateful for such a gift. Like that young girl, in my youth and early adulthood I attended daily Mass and many devotions but, as the demands of daily living increased, I became content with attendance at Sunday Mass and was satisfied with a quiet, intimate, personal relationship with God.

Attendance at large public prayer events were no longer part of my life. There were times in Medjugorje when I wished I could be more in tune with the big orchestra of prayer that touched me deeply but I felt myself reluctant to leave behind the safety of the silent informal relationship with God that I had chosen.

As I struggled with this feeling I came across some words of Archbishop Diarmuid Martin: 'Our relationship with Jesus cannot be just any kind of vague relationship in which I decide what Jesus would have done or do in my circumstance. A developed mature Christian faith requires knowledge of the scriptures.'

I think I began to understand something about the message of

Medjugorje. The message of Medjugorje is the same message as that of the gospels – peace and love. Again, like the girl in the story, I realised that I could have prepared better. If I was to make a fruitful journey as a pilgrim I should have started with the gospels and sought to deepen my relationship with God so that I could enter more fully into the spirit of Medjugorje. I have a lot to learn about the nature of pilgrimage. When I return to Medjugorje, which I hope to do some day, I hope, with God's help, to have opened my heart and my mind a little more.

The pilgrimage was not without its fun and laughter. The other guests in our house were delightful, funny, quick-witted but, above all, totally accepting. Christ must have been with us as I couldn't help thinking of his words: 'I come that you may have life and have it more abundantly.' I know I encounter him in the form of a beautiful young lady named Ruth. She heard me saying I was praying for someone who wished to become pregnant. Just before I left I realised that she had spent a lot of her time searching for a special prayer for this request and she had persevered until she found it. I should say one decade of the rosary every day for nine months and should find five people to say it with me. She immediately offered to be one of the five. What love I thought – to ask nothing for yourself but be so attentive to the needs of others. That, I think, was Medjugorje for me.

25

Fr Peter McAnenly

Fr Peter McAnenly was ordained a priest in June 1995 for the Archdiocese of Armagh. He is now Parish Priest of Eglish, Co. Tyrone and also Chaplain of two post primary schools in Dungannon and he has been the Director of Vocations for the diocese for the past year. From 1996 to 1997 he was based in the parish of Keady, Co. Armagh and it was during that year that he was introduced to Medjugorje.

This is Fr Peter's testimony.

I was first introduced to Medjugorje when I met the Cunningham family from Keady, Co. Armagh. I worked as a curate for one year in their parish and during that year Patrick Cunningham was tragically killed in America. It was through the tragedy of his death that I got to know the family very well. I spent a lot of time with them following Patrick's death trying to comfort and support them. During that time a great friendship was formed with Patrick's mother, Margaret, and her family; especially with her son Kevin and his wife Andrea and their family.

I was aware that Medjugorje played an important part in the life of the Cunningham family. I knew that it was a place that was special to them and it was a place where they had found great comfort and solace in the past and again after Patrick's death it was a place which helped them to come to terms with his passing.

Kevin asked me on a number of occasions to consider going to Medjugorje but, to be honest, I had no great desire to go as I had heard mixed reports about the place and, for different reasons, I was feeling a little bit uneasy or sceptical about the place. After some time, with much talk about it and a little bit of persuasion from Kevin Cunningham, I decided to go and experience the place for myself.

I went there on pilgrimage for the first time in 1998 and I went with an open heart and an open mind and I must say that I had a wonderful week. Martin Cunningham had organised a group of about forty people, who were largely from the parish of Keady. A number of the Cunningham family were also on the trip. There were many special and privileged moments during our days there, but above all else, it was a real retreat experience, a week of real peace and prayer. It was an opportunity to have some time out from the busyness of life and a time to reflect on one's own calling and situation in life.

I often say that a pilgrimage isn't just about place but it's also about people and Medjugorje was a place where I met the most incredible of people and in being there people felt secure enough to be open and honest and share the real story of their lives with one another. I often think of some of the wonderful people that I met during that week and some of the great conversations that I had with them and for some time to follow I maintained contact with a number of them.

During the week, I spent a lot of time with Kevin and another young man called Gavin and although we engaged in all the different pilgrimage activities with the group, the three of us went off and walked a lot and explored other places together. I remember the afternoon when we visited the beautiful Oasis of Peace and what a unique and peaceful place that was, a place where you could very much feel the nearness of God. I can also recall the afternoon when we visited the Cenacolo rehabilitation centre for young addicts with our group and how humbling it was to hear those men give their testimonies or share their stories.

Walking through the lovely vineyards, particularly at night, very often praying the rosary for a particular intention, was also special. As we walked there, what touched me was the poverty of the people, many of whom were there selling little crafts or little gifts which they had made, to help provide for their homes and for their families.

One of the key moments of each day was to join for the celebration of Mass each morning in the parish church and it was always unique to see the place packed with so many English-speaking people, so devoted and filled with such faith. What also enthused me was to see the huge numbers of people who were attending the sacrament of Reconciliation and very often the priest and penitent could be seen sitting under a tree with large queues of people standing by. As a priest, it was truly humbling to be able to celebrate the sacrament with so many people and it was wonderful to experience such quality confessions and to be able to offer the mercy of God.

I wasn't back in Medjugorje until 2011 and it was lovely to be able to go last year, with it being the 30th anniversary of the apparitions. In the thirteen years that passed between visits I have often wanted to return but, for many different reasons, it just didn't happen. Thirteen years may have passed but over those years I often thought of the place and it was still very much alive in my heart. From being there, I had known it to be a place with a difference, a place of real peace and joy and I was glad to have the opportunity to revisit it in 2011.

One of the things that occurs to me is that many people when speaking of Medjugorje speak of the visionaries and the daily apparitions but for me the story of the place is about something greater. Above all else, it is a place of living faith, a place where many go to be renewed in their faith and it is a place where many find comfort and healing and where people experience the nearness and the love of God.

When I was there last year, I could see many changes that had taken place since my previous visit.

One of the first things that struck me were the huge crowds of people and how the numbers had grown over the years. One of the lasting memories that I have from my 2011 visit is witnessing thousands of people quietly gathered outdoors each evening, perhaps up to 40,000 people gathered for Eucharistic Adoration. Many of these were young people. There we could see the Church alive; we could see it at its best; we could see people gathered day after day in large numbers giving praise and glory to God. What also struck me was the way in which the place itself had become more developed over the years and how it is now more prepared to deal with the growing number of pilgrims.

One of the added reasons that I went last year was because my father had passed away in the early part of the year and I felt that I would make the pilgrimage and offer it for him. As usual, we went out at about 5 a.m. on one of the mornings to climb the high mountain and what a spectacle of faith and fidelity that was. I also climbed it on two other occasions during the week by myself and I was glad to have the opportunity to do so, to give thanks for the gift of my father's life and to pray for the repose of his soul. Although I was very involved with our group, I managed to get plenty of time to myself and it was lovely just to find pockets of space and quiet to reflect on one's life and to pray for one's own personal needs.

A few days before going to Medjugorje last year I celebrated the funeral Mass of a lovely young girl called Sinead Rice-Arroita. I had celebrated the marriage of Sinead and her husband, Jorge, a few years earlier. She had been diagnosed with cancer a few years ago and Sinead had put up an incredible fight and was very determined to defeat her illness. She was a very inspiring and a very positive young woman and, over the years, I had gotten to know her very well and a special bond had developed, particularly as she fought her illness. A short time before Sinead's death Sr Briege McKenna, who is well known for her great healing work and ministry, had been in touch with her. They had prayed together on a few occasions by phone and I know that Sinead had found much support from Sr Briege. One of the mornings when I was at Mass in Medjugorje I met Sr Briege. She was there for a week-long retreat with a group of Irish women, a group who were beginning a new movement of prayer for women in Ireland. When I met her after Mass, I spoke for some time with her and I was able to tell her of Sinead's passing, which she was sorry to hear of. We spent a few minutes together talking about Sinead and sharing life with each other. It was a lovely privilege to have a few minutes praying with each other.

Towards the end of our week last year, a group of us went to the Blue Cross together. Again, it was special, walking through the vineyards in the quietness of the evening and remembering family and friends back home and praying for different needs and intentions. As I think of that evening, and, indeed, of many of the moments which I have had in Medjugorje, one of the lovely things about the place is just having quality time with people, to listen to them as they open up and share the story of their lives with you. That evening we spent a little time at the Blue Cross and then we climbed the small mountain in the dark of the night. I know that for those present that was one of the many highlights of our week as we sat at the cross up the mountain and looked out on the world below us. Just as the Apostles said to Jesus on that mountain top many years previously, 'It is good for us to be here.' Those same thoughts occurred to me and, indeed, those who were with us.

I led a short night prayer and we took some time to reflect on the Word of God, then everyone had an opportunity to share their own prayers and the intentions which lay close to their hearts. Again, it was a very privileged and prayerful moment and a moment when you really felt that God was near. I think that all of us wished we could have bottled up something of the spirit of that experience and taken it with us. Many of the group said to me afterward that it was such a wonderful experience for them that a large part of them didn't want to come down from the mountain! I must say that there have been times since then when I have had to face difficult situations in life and I have thought back to that night and it continues to enthuse and inspire me.

On the Friday evening of my pilgrimage, Ivan asked all of the priests who were in Medjugorje that week to join with him in the oratory at his home for an evening prayer. When I arrived, the oratory, which can accommodate about eighty people, was completely packed and it was only priests who were present, as well as Sr Briege McKenna. Given the fact that there were no seats left, I was asked to kneel at the front of the altar beside the place where Ivan was to kneel.

The prayers began at 6 p.m. and after praying the different prayers, we prayed the rosary together. At 6.40 p.m. Ivan had his apparition and I could only describe it as having been a very profound and powerful experience. As I've said, I was sitting next to him and for those few minutes, the room was completely silent and everyone's eyes were fixed on Ivan as he entered into that special moment. After his apparition, those present joined with him in praying the Magnificat together and then he conveyed to us the message which Our Lady had given in the apparition. As he spoke, two interpreters translated the message in both Italian and English.

Like most of the messages of Medjugorje, the message of that evening was a very simple one and, from what I can remember of Our Lady's message of that evening, she basically thanked the priests for the commitment of their lives. She went on to encourage priests to remain faithful to the Lord and to remain strong and constant in prayer.

It was a very unique and a very memorable experience and it was particularly special to be gathered in prayer with a large number of brother priests, praying for our own particular needs and for the needs of all priests.

There are many other things that I could say about Medjugorje and about some of the lovely experiences which I had there. I have just been there on two occasions and, God willing, I will return there in late August of 2012. I'm told that the number of people who will be travelling with our group has grown from last year and, interestingly, I spoke with someone last week who works in Medjugorje and he told me that the numbers in general this year are greater than last year, which says something about people's interest in and love for the place.

In conclusion, whilst there are many things that I like about the place and whilst there are many things that draw me back to it, one of the things which inspires me most of all is the sheer simplicity of the village. There we have simple people, living very simple lives and Our Lady enters into the midst of that simplicity on a daily basis to offer what can only be described as a very simple message and at the core of that message she challenges all of us to pray, to pray and to pray!

I'm confident that visiting Medjugorje has very much influenced my life and has coloured my ministry. I believe that Medjugorje is a place of living faith, a place of great healing and a place of great hope as we look to the future.